SMALL TEACHING ONLINE

———————————————

———————————————

EFFECTIVE STRATEGIES TO APPLY THE
SCIENCE OF LEARNING AND TO TEACH
ANYTHING WITHOUT ANY EFFORT.
A PRACTICAL GUIDE TO HAVING A
SUCCESSFUL AND EXCELLENT ONLINE
CLASS.

———————————————

———————————————

MACARENA TORRES

TABLE OF CONTENTS

INTRODUCTION

Internet learning is the freshest and most mainstream type of education and training today. In the previous decades, it has majorly affected postsecondary instruction, and the pattern is expanding, especially during the recent Covid-19 situation. During these changing times, a digital way of doing things has started to prevail in our everyday lives. The Internet has played a key role in the advent of such a digital education system. Through the Internet, students can access a vast amount of content, while interactive materials and methods also come into play.

When online, students are not bound to sit in the classroom and learn conventionally; instead, they can choose what they want to learn and what not to. On the Internet, everything is one click away, since you choose the topic, and everything is available at your fingertips. Video lectures are widely available for free on various streaming websites like YouTube, Vimeo, Dailymotion, and many more. Teaching Online also involves video conferencing with tools such as Zoom, Webex, and many more, making the lives of teachers easier.

While the Internet can be used for the general good, it can also be used for negative purposes such as spreading hatred or fake news. The authenticity of content is a big issue. Hence, this can have a very detrimental impact on young kids who are not in a position to distinguish what is right and wrong.

Overall, the Internet is an excellent education medium with many available websites on the Web providing certificates and relevant qualifications in any field of study.

Teaching is a great profession for personal development and can help us discover a huge amount about ourselves. It's a doorway to a better understanding of who we are because it exposes our flaws and forces us to look at the parts of ourselves we've been avoiding.

By reading this, you will be able to learn the different strategies and what you should know about online teaching. This will serve as a guide for you to know how to handle students in a virtual environment.

The internet gave us all access to anything from anywhere in the world at any time and changed the way that we thought. We were no longer reliant on someone to tell us what stories would be put under our nose; we could read and learn whatever we wanted and not be limited in sources. This took the blinders off the public when it came to finding out what was happening in the world and paved the way for modern learning and journalism.

Around the time that the internet was starting to grow in popularity with the general public, another invention was also first released and would change the way that the world functioned forever.

Online learning allows students to get much more out of the experience because they will be constantly engaged in the subject matter. Not only that, but it also means that anyone can enroll! Whether you recently graduated from high school, are a stay-at-home parent, or have been working for many years and are looking for a career change, online universities offer the freedom to be able to learn what you want when you want.

CHAPTER - 1

DESIGNING FOR LEARNING

Online education is not novel to students as much as it is to teachers. Many students are used to online courses. There are several online courses before the coronavirus came into the scene. Thus, you may not necessarily have any actions to take about preparing the students for online teaching. A survey carried out by the Babson Research Group claimed that around 33% of college students are engaged in at least one online course.

With this report, it is safe to say that you may not have any issues getting your students to learn. Another reason you don't necessarily have to take major move on your students is that most of them are conversant with the internet. They understand its workings. Thus, whatever platform you ask them to join will not be much difficult for them. Much of the work to get them ready for your classes depends on you. You need to do the following;

CREATE A COURSE GUIDE

You need to create a guide for your course for the students to see. The guide will contain the topics you will be treated with them; that is your class schedules. What you expect from your students and the period the lecture will run through.

MATERIAL AVAILABILITY

You need to ensure that your students have access to the materials they need for the course. This will help them adjust effectively to your online classes. They can't access you to get the materials for each course. So, you need to make a provision for them to have access to the materials.

UTILIZE EASY-TO-NAVIGATE PLATFORM

The platform you want to use for your classes should be easy to navigate. Make sure your students don't find it hard to come online and connect with you as you teach. This will help you get them available for every class.

CREATE MOBILE ACCESSIBILITY

One way to ensure that your students are well-positioned for your online teaching is to make the teaching accessible to them on their mobile phones. Make sure that the platform you adopt accepts mobile devices. This will make it easier for your students to connect with you anytime and anywhere.

Building your online classes requires you to make your students aware of how the course will run. Since you are about taking them online to teach, they need to be familiar with the process you want to use to teach them. Let them have access to the plan of the lessons. This way, they will easily blend into your online classes.

SETTING UP YOUR REMOTE LEARNING CURRICULUM

One possible question you will have on your mind right now is whether you have to change your current curriculum for remote learning. You don't have to change your current curriculum. Generally, the curriculum for the online school is always similar to that of traditional school. But there is a slight difference between them. The curriculum for the online school is often vast, giving the students access to many options to pick from. Also, the curriculum is set up flexibly, and it varies. This is what enables the students to learn at their own pace.

Also, many traditional schools are often limited by their budgets. Thus, they find it hard to provide the necessary materials and the teachers that will teach some of the topics in their curriculum. This often affects the quality of teaching materials made available for students. But as you go online, many tools will help you achieve a lot with your curriculum. You can easily get the result you want.

Rather than changing your curriculum, you will only work on it by adding fun-filled activities to it. The tools you will learn will aid you in adding interactive activities to your curriculum, which will help you to stimulate your student's minds and get them to learn effectively. By teaching your students online, your materials will be sourced from the internet, and many of them are free. This means your students will have access to more materials of study.

You will have to present your curriculum in multiple formats for your students to gain from. The formats include creating your curriculum in a direct-instruction video and using interactive learning tools such as audiobooks, etc. Also, you can create back up for your courses so that your students can easily come back and listen to them.

You don't have to change your current curriculum. You only need to work more on it to make it more effective for your students. Online classes will give you enough flexibility to set up your curriculum. Utilize all of this flexibility to your advantage, and you will get the best result. Stay active, and you will have a lot to gain.

CHAPTER - 2

WAYS TO PREPARE
YOUR COURSE

CHOOSE YOUR TOPIC

Start by making a list of all the things that you know how to do. Don't leave anything out. You'll be surprised at the volume of ideas you have. Try to write 100 ideas. It could be anything – this is just a brainstorm of ideas to get the ball rolling.

Ask yourself these questions:

- What do your friends say that you are good at? If you don't know, ask them.

- What do people ask you to help them with? Think about the value you bring to others.

- If people are already asking you about it, is there a potential market for you to tap into?

- Is there a subject area of your profession that is complex, misunderstood, or could be presented in a new way?

- What special skills do you have that you could teach someone else about?

- What unique experiences do you have that might help someone else?

Many people get stuck choosing a topic because they're not sure if they're "expert enough" for the topic. They often lack the confidence to think they could teach others about the subject. If you feel this way, remember that you have a message to share! You simply need to be further ahead on the journey than others are. Think about where you were yesterday and where you are today. Many of your learners will be where you were yesterday, and you can help them get to where they need to be today. Helping your students move from one stage to another is your goal. This facilitates change, and that's the goal for any course.

Once you get your list together, you'll have something to work with. Start to eliminate the ideas that seem boring, uninteresting, or that just don't interest you enough. Slowly begin to narrow down the list until you have four or five topics that excite you. Then make a final decision on your topic.

WILL PEOPLE BUY THIS?

Once you've narrowed down your topic, you'll want to take some time to do some market research. Ask yourself these questions:

Would someone pay money for this topic?

Is there a demand for it?

Are there any other courses out there on this topic?

If you can't find any other courses on this topic, you may want to choose another subject. There's probably a reason why there aren't any courses out there on this subject. Remember, competition is good! It means there is a demand for what you want to teach. It means people are paying for it. That means there's room for you too!

Remember, the style someone else has when teaching something will be different than the style in which you teach it! Everybody is different. Here are some questions to help you define how you're different. Your answers will help you describe your special self.

- What matters most to you?

- What are five to ten random facts about you?

- What are some of your pet peeves?

WHO IS YOUR AUDIENCE?

If you take the time to research your audience, you'll ensure your course has value to your students. You must thoroughly understand your audience and their potential learning goals. You need answers to these questions:

- What do they need to learn?

- What are their interests?

- What are their experience levels?

- What is their educational level?

WHAT ARE YOUR COURSE OBJECTIVES?

People don't buy ideas; they don't buy a course. They buy transformation and change. They want to get from Point A to Point B. Your course must address the needs and pain points of your ideal student. That's why your course must have specific, measurable learning outcomes.

You must define what you want your course to accomplish. If you begin with the end in mind, you'll stay on topic as you write your course. Your potential students will know exactly what they'll learn from your course. You can also use these objectives to write your course introduction and course sales page.

Write down your answers to these important questions:

- What specific problem will your course solve?

- What change will happen as a result of taking your course?

- What new skills, attitudes, or behaviors will your students be able to demonstrate?

- Why should they take your course?

- What do you want your students to achieve by taking your course? What is your dream for them?

You can then use your answers to the above questions to write your learning outcomes. You'll want to write sentences that describe an action of what specifically the student will be able to do. For example, "By the end of this course, you'll be able to cook a gourmet dinner from start to finish."

OUTLINE YOUR PLAN

Taking the knowledge out of your head and organizing the framework of your course can seem overwhelming at first. You might be asking yourself some of these questions:

"I have a topic, but how do I break it up?"

"I don't want to leave anything out, but I'm not sure what to talk about first."

"How do I talk about all this without being boring?"

The best way to start - is to just start!

An easy way to get started organizing your content is to just take your knowledge from your head to paper. Just does a brain dump and get everything on paper.

From there, you'll begin to organize and clearly outline every piece of content, learning outcome, and the lesson that you'll teach. This outline will eventually become your course topics and subtopics.

From your outline, you'll create every module and lesson title. Once your course is complete, you'll write a summary of each lesson. You'll use these later when you're selling your course and offering free samples of your course.

DETERMINE YOUR COURSE MODULES

Think about where your course is going. From your outline, decide on what exactly you're planning to cover. Start by determining the scope of your topic. Then pick the larger subtopics - these will be your course modules. For example, if you were creating a course on "Making Delicious Dinners," the subtopics could be Salads, Soups, and Main Dishes. The subtopics are your modules.

CREATE YOUR COURSE LESSONS

From there, each module will be further broken down into lessons. This is where the actual content of your course will be located. You'll include any video, pdf files, audio files, etc. into each lesson.

Let's continue with our course on "Making Delicious Dinners." In the module on "Salads," you might have three different lessons: Spinach Salad, Garden Salad, and Caesar Salad. The main idea is to create your modules and then break them down into lessons - keeping each lesson very specific.

BEST LENGTH FOR THE LECTURES

In today's world, attention spans are getting shorter. People now have access to quick information available on the internet. This makes us impatient with anything that doesn't quickly get to the point and offer extreme value. This is good news for creating an online course because you can reduce any extraneous content and get right to the information. Depending on the subject and how engaging you can make it, the general rule is between about three to seven minutes. That said, there's no hard and fast rule for how long a lesson should be - it's more important for it to be active, engaging, and transforming.

HOW WILL STUDENTS ACCESS YOUR COURSE?

Once your course is complete, you'll determine how students will access your course.

In addition to providing ways to author and assemble courses, marketplace platforms provide an existing marketplace where you can sell online courses.

HOST YOUR OWN PLATFORMS

These platforms are geared towards subject matter experts or small businesses who want a relatively easy way to set up their own branded site where they can sell their courses. There are small differences between each of these options, such as the resources they provide, support, and educational content. Research the various sites, their pricing plans, and features to determine which is best for you. Many of these platforms offer free trial options.

BUILD IN WAYS TO ESTABLISH RAPPORT WITH YOUR STUDENTS

The most successful online courses empower students and allow them to openly communicate with the instructor. So how do you create an open environment in an online class since you're not meeting face to face? How do you make sure students are willing to talk to you?

You must establish rapport early. You must help your students feel comfortable, confident, and valued by you. Here's how:

HOW MUCH CONTENT DO I NEED FOR MY COURSE?

This is a tough one as every course is different, and there are several things to take into account. The topic of the course, the audience and their behavior, the types of media that your audience is used to learning with, and much more. If you are creating a session on 'How to Cook a Roast Turkey' you may be looking at creating a lot less content than if you were teaching 'AngularJS for Beginners.'

Start by outlining each of the critical topics in your course. Break this information down into a series of modules, taking into account that each module should take no more than 11 minutes to complete to coincide with the attention span of your learners. Once you have this list, you can then see how many modules you will need to create content for within your course. An excellent bite-sized learning course needs to be precisely that, bite-sized. However, with more complex subjects that require a deeper level of detail, you can push out to a maximum of between one to two hours' worth of content, with six to 12 modules to break the content into easily digestible portions.

WHAT SHOULD MY CONTENT INCLUDE?

Now that you know what you are trying to achieve in each one of your modules; the next step is building your learning content. There's a vast range of ways that you can do this, and the driving factor behind it lies within your audience. Every audience will respond to different types of content differently, so this should determine the first step in how you will present your modules to your learners. Having said this, the most effective way to get the maximum engagement out of learners is to present your content by using a variety of mediums, including interactive or immersive elements, where possible. For those new to creating content, some of the most popular ways to include content within online learning are:

- Video
- Interactive SCORM files

- Audio files

- Image based documents and slides

Ensuring that your message is clear so that learners can quickly and easily understand learning concepts is critical, regardless of the presentation medium. But now we will take a closer look at each of these popular ways of delivering content so that you can get the best engagement result possible.

Length of Videos

When it comes to creating video content for online courses, the length of the video is critical in learning engagement and knowledge retention. Jumping back to the micro-learning concept: short videos are much more effective for participation, and for allowing students to absorb the content. So how long should videos be?

There are numerous studies on this exact topic, with the optimal time coming in at between four to six minutes. The team at edX has completed one of the most recent studies relating to video consumption in education, and they have revealed some fascinating findings. The optimal video length is six minutes. While students watch most of the way through videos at this length, once you exceed that period, engagement drops off like walking off a cliff.

For all videos over six minutes, less than one-third of the content viewed is retained. In cases where a student is in a certificate-based course, due to that added commitment involved, this engagement time is prolonged to 12 minutes. The clear message from these studies is that content creators should be breaking their material up into bite-sized pieces to maximize student engagement.

Interactive Content for Learning

Video is excellent, but getting your learners interacting with your content is even better! Creating interactive content for the sake of interaction is not the solution, though. Sometimes letting a learner absorb information can be better than sending a user on a clicking spree. By understanding what interactivity means in learning, you can find the right balance for maximum engagement without resulting in distraction. The best way to understand interactive content is by contrasting it with real-life or face-to-face social interaction.

Creating an experience in which an interaction results in a response, in the same way that a conversation flows, is the key to building a free-flowing online learning experience. As mentioned above, forcing a learner into a click frenzy is one of the worst things that you can do. Excessive clicking leads to learner fatigue, which in turn provides more of a distraction to the learner than anything else. In such a case, the focus is more on clicking through all of the content rather than engaging with it.

Get the Learner Thinking, and then Clicking to Promote Deep Thinking

Allowing your learners to think, reflect, and feel the content is also a much-overlooked aspect of interactive content creation. Stacking content that is forcing learners to push through everything at a rapid pace creates a rushed and stressful experience. By creating space in the material, learners can take a step back, reflect on the content, understand what they have experienced, and achieve a greater grasp of the content before moving on to the next module. As you can't simulate a truly immersive interactive role-playing environment, think of ways in which you can get the learner to do something similar within your course. Allow your users to start practicing the skills right away. Creating scenarios based on achieving goals is a simple way of getting started with this.

Mix It Up!

Whichever path you choose to go down when creating your content, there is something important to remember; switch it up! Yes, video is great, but an entire course of the only video will be horrible for engagement. Include a range of media in your class. This may be a mix of written material, video, interactive content, audio, and images. Not every module needs to have all of these elements. However, if you **create** a flow between them over the length of the entire course, you will find that learners will absorb a lot more of the content and be a lot more competent in applying their new skills in real-life scenarios.

HOW TO TEST YOUR LEARNERS?

So, your learners have completed their course, now what is the best way to test them? The most common online course assessment tool is a multiple-choice quiz and 'match the answer' type of questions. But these may not be the best solutions for you. Getting a little more creative with how you assess your students may provide a better form of measurement of success in your field. Short and long-form answers are also great but can be time-consuming as an assessor. Why not let technology make that more comfortable for you? Try out some new tools to save time and ensure that your learners are paying attention.

Video response questions, and to a lesser extent, audio response questions, are great for this. Not only can the assessor quickly and easily view and grade long-form answers, but they can also see and hear students while responding! As with content, changing things up is critical to engagement and getting the students to think in a range of ways as they respond. Hit them with the multiple-choice questions in the early modules, and then wrap up the course with a longer-form video response question or more extended form style of response.

TRACKING PROGRESS

Hosting your course within a learning management system allows you to track your learners' every move. See how people are interacting with content. If they are dropping out, see where the dropout occurs. If you have multiple courses, you can track enrollments. Most importantly, you can use the system to trigger email reminders and congratulation notifications as users hit milestones throughout the process.

HOW DO I KNOW IF MY CONTENT IS ANY GOOD?

Get some coworkers or friends to take the course so that they provide you with feedback. Encourage them to take notes as they complete the course, so that you know which elements might need tweaking, rearranging, or removing to create a better learning experience. Another great way to test out your course is to release it as a Beta version to a small group of potential students. If you are charging money for the course, you may offer it for free to a limited number, which is then required to provide feedback on the process.

The most valuable feedback you can get is from those who will be completing the course, so the more information you can get from your users, the better. After launching to the public, another great initiative to include is following up with all students after they have completed the course. This way, you can get their feedback around how you might be able to improve the course. All of this feedback helps you to develop and improve your content continually, so you can attract more users and provide a more rounded and engaging learning experience.

CHAPTER - 3

GUIDING LEARNING THROUGH ENGAGEMENT

ENGAGING STUDENTS IN LEARNING

We all seek to figure out what is the easiest and most practical way to teach each of our courses. If you conclude that you want to pursue some synchronous teaching at least and probably keep office hours with Zoom, below are some helpful ideas for pedagogy.

Manage Participants

If you click at the bottom of the screen on "Manage Participants" (you might have to hover over it), the names of the participants will appear on the right. Participants have the choice to provide input that will help you control the speed of understanding.

(Yes, No, Go Faster, Go Slower, etc.) After resetting, the host can press "Delete Everything." This is a perfect way to do a quick check-in without using polling instruments!

Whiteboard

You can consume it on your own or allow students to use it with each other or with you. Mostly it is anonymous participation except for the arrow, which will have the name of the student on it (though not yours)—the text size defaults to 24.

You may want to make it 18 depending on the operation so that you can fit more responses from the students on the whiteboard. Here are some ways to use the whiteboard interactively: You can type in an open-ended question and ask students to reply on the whiteboard to start a discussion or reading about a subject.

"What if..." With each quadrant, you can draw a grid asking students to consider another dimension of an item, possibly as a pre-assessment of their awareness of a new topic. Students type their answers into the relevant quadrant. After a simulation of operation, you can use it as a space for reflection.

You can conclude your class with either a Whiteboard or Chat question that helps you and them measure and reinforce your learning. For example, students may respond to the following three questions on three separate parts of the whiteboard: What do you now know you didn't do an hour ago? What would you do now that, an hour ago, you couldn't? What would you tell a peer you wouldn't be able to do an hour ago? The host will save a Whiteboard picture as a record of the discussion that you can share directly with the students or put into Canvas, but it won't be collected automatically.

Check-ins and breaks

It is called a film strip when the faces of the participants appear linear, and fewer participants will be visible. It can be changed, so participants turn up in a grid format (Brady Bunch style).

Either way, if your course is significant, then not everybody will appear, and at the same time, everybody's face would not be visible to you. Try to click through the faces of the participants as much as possible to try to decide whether they are engaged.

Mind to check in daily. Start the meeting 10 minutes early so students can either speak or use the chat to communicate as they would usually do before class.

Getting it to Stick

Something that we all want to be creating is sticky learning. For those of you who haven't heard that term before, it means that your learners are interacting with your learning content and remembering the information. Peter C. Brown et al, in their book Make it Stick, provided some effective strategies that make learning easier. While engagement occurs when learners interact with the content while completing your course, sticky learning is about having learners remember the content after completing your course. Sticky learning is the goal for any teacher, as it means that your students are not just skimming through content; they are ingesting and understanding it at the same time. This then allows them to apply their learning to real-life situations, and isn't this why we are taking courses in the first place?

Success in education doesn't necessarily mean that you have to walk away with a mastered skill. Something that could be seen as even more valuable is that your learners walk away with a positive behavioral change or thought process. After all, sticky learning that doesn't result in a change in behavior isn't any more useful than something that doesn't stick at all!

So how do we develop learning materials that result in sticky learning? Extensive research on education best practices has revealed the following.

Provide meaningful learning

By providing learning experiences that are meaningful for learners, students can remain engaged and take ownership of the learning experience. Ideally, the learning process should have significant real-life applications. Therefore, students should be presented with learning scenarios that speak to them.

Allow learners to share knowledge and experiences

As mentioned above, learners must take ownership of the learning process. What better way to do this by involving them in such a process as much as possible? Another effective way to do so is to allow students to share their knowledge and personal experiences, which will make learning very meaningful to them.

Offer interactive learning experiences

The learning process should be as interactive as possible. There is nothing wrong with a conventional education model, yet it is a fact that learners' interest will be greatly aroused when participating in a very interactive lesson that entails real-life applications.

Provide support and encourage discussion

Since learning is a very 'personal' process, which takes place inside our brains, it is a proven fact that every one of us learns in a different way and at a different pace. That means during a lesson, there might be learners that are left behind, which eventually causes them to become disengaged. Hence, the educator has to provide the appropriate support throughout the learning process and instigate an active discussion. An active discussion will also enhance peer learning (i.e. learning from classmates) that sometimes can be even more effective.

Initiate a post-learning experience

Have you noticed what all companies that excel in customer service have in common? It's after-sales service. On a similar note, just delivering an outstanding lesson is not effective on its own. There needs to be a reinforcement of the concepts taught as well as some kind of support from the educator to the learner. Although it may not be possible for the educator to immediately respond to every query that a learner might have after the lesson, there can be some form of a post-learning experience, which will benefit both students and teachers. Such an experience would indicate how concepts have been applied in real-life situations and collect feedback on the learning process, making it even more effective.

Share results or success stories

Student motivation is essential in the learning process. By sharing past results or success stories of other learners, learners can become more motivated and confident in achieving the course or lesson objectives.

There is nothing new about any of these items we have talked about here. They are all things that we should already be doing, but sometimes we can get caught up in the learning material and forget that this is about the learner and not just the content. Hopefully, by keeping these details in mind, you can create a more rounded and sticky experience for your next course.

Bite-Sized Learning

Some new buzzwords have been coming up in the online learning community lately. 'Bite-sized learning' or 'microlearning' have both been the latest rage as the online learning platforms have increased in popularity over the past few years. But for many newcomers to the online learning world, you may not understand precisely what these terms mean, or how you can incorporate them into your programs. The short answer is that bite-sized learning is about breaking up your course or learning program, into a series of smaller, more manageable modules. This allows the learner to complete the course in short bursts, rather than having to spend hours at a time working on a particular part of their course.

In the age of modern technology, people no longer want to spend hours on end sitting at a computer working through a course. Instead, they would much prefer to be able to access their learning materials via a mobile device or tablet so they can learn at times that suit them while they are in transit, waiting for an appointment, or simply when they don't feel like sitting at a computer. The learning retention levels for bite-sized courses are much higher due to the shorter length of the content, and the ability for learners to retain information is increased, as they are not being overloaded with information in one go. If you are still not convinced that bite-sized learning is the way to go when creating your next course, let's take a look at some of the stats.

Tips for Putting Together Your Bite-Sized Learning Course

Now that you have seen how important is microlearning let's look at how you should be structuring your content for the most engagement.

Stick to One Idea

The idea of creating content in a bite-sized format allows the learner to pick up a new skill in a short space of time. To keep things simple and on track, ensure to only focus on one idea in each course. If you want to run through a new idea, create a new course for that. By keeping the focus of your content in one area, you can teach your learners much more quickly and efficiently.

Engage

Just because your course is short, it doesn't mean that it shouldn't be engaging. If you start including sub-par content, your learners will be zoned out in no time. Kick-off your course with engaging content and finish it with engaging content while keeping it consistent with no 'filler' material in between.

Keep the Content Relevant

Further to the above information about engagement, it's important to keep your content relevant. This is bite-sized learning; you don't need to drag your points out. Keep your learning content simple and direct, and your learners will be picking it up and understanding it a lot faster.

Be Smart When Grouping Your Content

Each module that you create should be focusing on a particular area within the core topic of the course. When creating your modules, it's critical to group your content in the correct module to ensure that the learning sticks with other materials that it is relevant to. Here are some additional tips on grouping your content:

- Decide the one learning result you wish to accomplish.

- Determine the tasks that are related to this one goal.

- Distinguish content that is pertinent to this one learning objective.

- Arrange the content into nuggets.

- Include information that tests students for information and abilities they acquired and anticipated to demonstrate in the application.

Keep It in Context

As a content creator, your job is to present information that your learners can use. You can provide content with value and boost engagement by providing relevant content. You must state plainly the course objectives at the beginning of the course. Then you should fill your module with solutions. Illustrate to the learners the means they could resolve their real difficulties. Last but not least, use the assessment tools to test learners for knowledge and skills that they will have to apply when they use such knowledge in the real world.

Create A Learner Driven Experience

The reason that you create learning content is so that your learners can learn, so why wouldn't you let your learner drive their learning experience. Give them the flexibility to determine when and where they want to learn. Create your content using a learning management system with a user-friendly and intuitive layout that lets the learner explore resources and discover content on their own and don't forget to make it fun!

AVAILABLE ONLINE TOOLS FOR MAINTAINING STUDENT ENGAGEMENT

There is a vast array of tools that can be used to aid learning. These tools have been created to give autonomy to students, to improve the need for collaboration, to enhance communication during online learning between the teacher and the students, and to aid the administration of online directives. In this chapter, I will be touching on some of the tools you can rely on to achieve the purpose of your online teaching. Please note that the list is not exhaustive, as there are so many online tools out there.

Socrative

Socrative is a product of some set of entrepreneurs and engineers who have been highly interested in education. It is designed to help teachers create educational exercises or games. These games are designed in such a way that they can be solved with mobile devices or laptops. The teacher has access to the results of the exercises and games, and this gives him or her the ability to modify the activity or games to be more personalized to the students.

Participate

It gives the teacher the ability to gather information from the internet and distribute it to members of the groups. It provides the teacher with the possibility to manage the academic content found online, which will, in turn, improve the research skills and assist in monitoring the achievements of students during a course. Also, participate offers the possibility of setting up a class virtually and making a portfolio in which all work can be stored.

Animoto

With Animoto, the teacher can easily create HD videos using any mobile device. These videos can serve various functions, such as inspiring the students and helping them to improve their learning. Animoto is designed with a comfortable and friendly interface. It is also practical by allowing teachers to make audiovisual content that will work correctly for educational needs.

Kahoot!

This is a very popular classroom platform for taking quizzes, which come in the form of games. It allows teachers to create discussions, questionnaires, or surveys that can be used alongside their lessons. The content produced is displayed to the students for answers. Kahoot is designed to promote learning through games. The principal purpose is to increase the engagement of students and come up with an educational environment that is dynamic and social as well as fun at the same time.

Several online tools are available to help students learn online in a fun way from home. By being familiarized with these tools as an educator, the students' online learning experience can become intriguing and insightful.

CHAPTER - 4

SURFACE BACKWARD DESIGN

I f the challenges of online teaching and the introduction to small teaching have shown us anything, it is that for instructors to excel as online tutors, they need to explore teaching plans that are simple and allow them to meet the learning needs of the students without overburdening them with work. You need to bring small teaching into the teaching plan you are designing for your students, and this is where backward design comes in.

Backward design is a technique for creating teaching plans by defining goals before selecting ways of evaluating learning and teaching strategies.

The idea of backward design is to focus your teaching on learning goals, which usually ensures that what you are teaching your students is well organized and suited for their learning needs. Simply put, the backward design requires that you begin with understanding the goal of the course or program that your students will learn and focusing on imparting the knowledge that your students need to have before you decide how you will evaluate their learning to show that they have learned what is necessary. And then decide how best to teach them to be better equipped to meet the evaluation criteria.

IN THEORY

The backward design takes a holistic approach to the process of learning, and it encourages you as an instructor to focus on how learning exercises and assessments ensure that the course objectives are achieved. The backward design allows teachers to figure out which materials are essential for students to achieve the expressed learning goals. This makes it easier for you to choose what to add to the learning curriculum and what to leave out. It is also making the learning process more productive as your students would be able to focus on the things that matter. It makes it easier for you to determine the ideal student learning results, evaluate these results, and determine the classroom exercises and related course materials that are expected to obtain these results. Another advantage of using the backward design is that students value less complicated learning. When you share course objectives clearly with your students, they will understand what is expected of them and work towards achieving these objectives. Teaching using backward design gives both the students and instructors greater clarity.

When designing a course, there are three important questions you need to ask yourself to ensure that you are following a backward design approach. These questions are:

1. What do I want my students to be able to do at the end of the course? This addresses the learning goals and objectives for the course.

2. How will I measure if my students can do that? This enables you to develop a streamlined method of assessment.

3. How will I get my students ready for the assessment? This enables you to put together a teaching plan or curriculum.

Creating great learning objectives through clear statements that tell your students the skills and knowledge they are expected to have at the end of the course is the first step in the backward design process.

The next step is deciding how you will measure the skills and knowledge based on the learning objectives you have created. Whatever method of assessment you pick should be appropriate for the course and tailored to clearly show their understanding of the important parts of what they are learning. Also, each assessment you give should be suited to their level. For example, if the topic you are creating an assessment for is an introductory level topic, its objectives are bound to concentrate on remembering past knowledge, understanding the basic concepts of the new topic, and linking past knowledge to the basic concepts of the new topic. As such, assignments and tests that focus on asking students to remember old knowledge, answering questions about basic concepts, and linking both old knowledge and the new basic concepts together, are appropriate.

Finally, you can now design streamlined training modules for the course. Your training modules should be custom fitted to guarantee that students are prepared for assessments. Your teaching modules should also be engaging because the more engaged your students are, the more chances they will have to learn.

MODELS

The backward design approach has three stages. These stages are defining the desired results, deciding proof of desired results, and planning learning modules and experiences.

Defining the Desired Results

The big picture that you feel is important for your students to have regardless of whether they remember anything else from your course or not is what we are discussing here. This big picture can stand out from the vast range of information you think the students should have about the topic or course. The big picture is the focal point your students need to understand. Without this big picture, the course, module, or other learning material would be pointless. Taking a model from this chapter, the big picture is that you understand how backward design learning works.

How to define the desired outcomes:

1. Identify the big picture.

2. Concentrate on the big picture.

Deciding Proof of Desired Results

Assessment is the invisible finish line on your students' "race" to learning. It is what proves that both you and your students have reached the finish line of the particular topic or course and that everyone has achieved the specified objectives. It is up to you to figure out what that finish line will be. What is sufficient proof of your students' understanding and mastery of the topic or course? Is it getting at least 70% or 80% in an assessment test or as a total in a group of assessment exercises, including tests, an examination, gradable term papers, and group projects?

How to decide proof of desired results:

1. Decide satisfactory levels of proof that showing you and your students have reached the ideal outcomes.

2. Create finish line assessment tests and a range of evaluation techniques (assignments, tests, projects, and so on.)

Planning Learning Modules and Experiences

When you are planning and designing your instructional materials, there are a few elements you should consider. You should structure your learning modules and learning experiences in a way that allows your students to know how each learning material is related to the general objective, how it expands on their earlier information, and what is required of them to successfully finish the module and show mastery of the learning materials. The learning modules or experiences should also be related to their interest or be flexible enough for them to personalize it. In conclusion, the direction you pick should give your students chances to gain mastery of the course and to review their growth.

How to plan learning modules and experiences:

1. Design exercises that will cause desired outcomes to occur.

2. Focus on information and skills that students should acquire to have the ideal outcomes

PRINCIPLES

One of the fundamental objectives of designing learning situations using backward design learning principles is to deliver learning experiences that are suitable for your students. Ideally, the learning conditions you create should be flexible and should allow all your students to take part in the learning process in ways that address their issues.

By giving students alternatives in learning and exhibition of their learning, you emphasize flexibility that supports a mixed range of learning material as opposed to just sticking to what one textbook or reading material says. This way, your students will have a better chance at learning because the materials they choose are suited to cater to their learning needs. When relying primarily on traditional teaching methods and following textbooks' letters, your alternatives (in learning materials and exercises) are frequently constrained to what the book offers. However, when teaching for understanding, you are just constrained by what your students should achieve before the end of the teaching session. When you use backward design learning principles, your students have alternatives by the way they learn, how they express what they have learned, and how they modify their learning to accommodate their interests and learning goals.

Teaching towards the understanding of the big picture rather than covering the material out of a picked course material gives you greater flexibility and gives your students more chances to learn. This is the focal principle of backward design. The backward design encourages students to concentrate on, and connect with, the learning objectives.

This brings us to another key principle of Backward Design: planning. To successfully use the backward design structure, you need to plan your objectives. If you want your students to leave the learning session with a good understanding of the big picture and key ideas, you need to factor in enough time into your course for them to connect and relate with the major ideas in different ways. Spend more time with them on the major ideas and less time on the minor ideas.

Another principle of backward design is that it enables you to ask (and answer) some significant questions concerning your students' learning. These questions include:

- Is the learning module I created impactful, or is it just strong enough to catch my students' interest briefly?

- How will I know that my students have gained an understanding of the subject matter?

Using the backward design structure is like embarking on a journey. At the start of your journey, the goal at the top of your priority list is your destination, and you need to figure out a schedule that allows you to get there. You also need to design metrics that allow you to judge if you have gotten to your destination or not. It is as simple as this.

Regardless of whether you are designing a talk, an entire course, or some other instructional material, you can use Backward Design principles to assist you with staying on target while addressing the greatest questions that your students will need you to answer in due order regarding what you are teaching: "what really matters?"

SMALL TEACHING ONLINE QUICK TIP: SURFACE BACKWARD DESIGN ONLINE

In terms of small teaching online, backward design is one of the best ways to break down online teaching into small bits that can make it easier for you to teach students in ways that will have long-lasting effects. Backward design online follows the general steps for traditional physical learning.

Identify Desired Outcomes

In doing this, some important questions need to be posed. These questions include:

1. What would you like your students to take home from the teaching?

2. What is the desired outcome or aim of each lesson and the overall learning plan?

For example, let's say you are teaching a course on nutrition. The three focal points of a nutrition course are understanding concepts about nutrition, understanding how people can get the most nutrition out of their meals, and understanding eating patterns.

Using the aforementioned questions, you will most likely arrive at the desired outcome like this: At the end of the course, students should be able to use their knowledge of nutrition to design meals that enable them and others to get the best nutrition considering different eating patterns.

Determine Worthy Proof

It is not just enough to identify the outcome you want. You need to have a measurement system that allows you to identify worthy proof that the desired outcome has been achieved. Tests and assignments can be great measurement systems.

Using the aforementioned example, worthy proof would be a test in which the students put together a one-week meal plan for a family making use of the lessons they have been taught. The objective is a delicious and healthy meal plan.

Plan Learning Encounters and Guidance

As an instructor, you should first consider the skills and knowledge your students will require to complete the assessment test or assignment.

Based on the aforementioned example, students would need to be informed about various nutritional categories, human nutrition requirements (proteins, carbohydrates, sugars, minerals, vitamins, and so on.), and about what food sources give these requirements.

Your teaching techniques should include personal one-on-one communication between you and your students and inductive strategies, as well as group exercises, which can be done through online platforms like Zoom.

In backward design, you begin with objectives, then you create or plan out assessments, and finally, you create the learning modules and experiences. Here, you pick the goal first and use it as a guide to design the process to reach that goal. This will help your students stay focused and committed to the course work because there is an endpoint in sight, and even if the big picture seems large when broken down into modules and lessons to grasp it, it becomes very easy to understand.

CHAPTER - 5

HOW TO GET YOUR

ONLINE CLASS STARTED

SELECTING YOUR TRIBE

Who are you're target students? It is the first question you should meditate before creating your online course. It seems difficult but not impossible to know the target students that you want to teach.

Knowing the tribe will help you to understand how broad your industry will be. Let's take, for example, if you are planning to teach music lessons, you know that your tribe will be young adults who want to enroll in a music lesson. Your tribe is the specific set of individuals that you are looking forward to joining in your online class.

These sets of individuals might be broad, like in the case of web developers, or it can be narrow like in the case of cake makers.

To know the specific set of people to teach, you should do the following;

Online research

Run online research to see the number of people that are interested in your course. Another easy way is social media groups like WhatsApp groups, Facebook groups. You will be able to interact with students and know what they are looking for in a course. Not only that, but you will also be able to understand how to create your course to suit your audience.

Visiting Schools

That might look awkward, most especially if you are a shy type of person. Don't worry; I will teach you how to communicate effectively in the latter part of this book. Visiting schools will give you the avenue to interact with students and know the significant courses they are finding it difficult. From there, you can be able to create your course on such subjects.

Attending Seminar's

You could be opportune to see a large congregation of students in a seminar, and you will be able to interact with them and know their major problems.

Attending seminars does not only helps you to understand your target students, but it is also an avenue to market your course.

There are still other ways that you can determine your target audience. You can think of a better way of knowing who your target audience is and how to reach out to them.

Let me put you through some benefits of knowing your tribe;

Knowing your tribe will help you to;

Market your online school

You will be able to promote your school online if you know the specific set of people that you are targeting.

Branding your online school

You will be able to give your school a unique identity if you know who you're target audience is and their locations.

Pricing your course

You will also be able to understand how to price your course so that it will be affordable to the students. You will not like to set a price that will scare your students. You will want something that your students can afford easily.

Creating course contents

Like I said earlier, determining your audience will be crucial in your course creation. It will help you to know how to tailor your course so that your audience will understand it.

Your audience will determine how effective your online course will be and how profitable it will be.

You might be wondering how you could be able to handle students that have language barrier issues. I will put you through how to handle students with diverse language in the latter part of this book.

Can you answer these questions:

· Who is my target audience?

- Which country is your audience located?

- Do we have the same time zone?

- What is the age range of my target audience?

The answer to these questions will help you a lot in narrowing down your target audience.

Now that we know our audience. Let now get to the main work.

ACTIVE LEARNING STRATEGIES FOR STARTING CLASS

The learning activity can jump-start class by immediately putting students into the driver's seat of their learning. It's also a powerful way to get a sense of their prior learning so that you can calibrate your instruction to the specific needs of the class. Additionally, active learning, using specific methods, such as In the News or the Sticky Scenario, can be effective ways to establish the relevance of the subject matter.

Polls

Because the polling tool is built into Zoom, it is relatively easy to set up and employ. Use polls to test comprehension by opening class with a quick, 3 to 5-question, ungraded quiz. Design these quizzes to assess whether or not students grasp the main concepts in the required reading or other preassigned material. Another approach is to create a short scenario and require students to choose from a multiple-choice list of possible solutions.

Bring Questions

Ask your students to prepare for class by bringing a question that emerged from their reading or perhaps from work on a major paper or project. Invite your students to interject questions when they are most pertinent to the current material. This method is best used throughout the class period but can be a great way to start class. It gets the session underway with an inquiry mindset instead of an information mindset.

In the News

Before class, your students search the news using keywords related to the class topic. Begin the class by asking a few students to screen share an article, provide a summary, and explain its connection to the material. Alternatively, place students in small groups and have them share their findings. Visit some of the groups so that you are aware of the articles and make reference to them during your instruction.

Define Success

Provide your students with an outline for the class session, put them in breakout groups, and ask them to discuss, "What would make today's class a success for you?" Or make this an individual reflection with the following instructions, "Take 2-3 minutes to review the outline and get a sense of what we'll address today. Then write out a personal learning goal." Defining the goal helps students to personalize and take ownership of their role in the learning process.

Comprehension Test

Comprehension tests are similar to polling but graded. One of my graduate school professors used this method for every class. He began class with a 12-15 question quiz on the core concepts of our assigned reading. When complete, we would review the questions and correct answers. During the review, he opened the floor for clarifying questions, and he would lecture only on the material that needed further explanation, ideas we wanted to explore, or theories we didn't yet understand. While Zoom polls can record individual answers, it's a lot of work to get poll results out of Zoom and into your LMS for grading. Instead, I recommend you use the quiz module built into your LMS. These quiz modules have more robust question features, review options, and the grades will go directly into your online grade book.

Prior Knowledge Survey

Prior knowledge surveys differ from polls because they require students to write or type short essay-type responses. The most straightforward method is to give students 2-3 minutes to write out everything they already know about a topic. You can stop there, or ask them to elaborate, going beyond the reading to make connections with their life experience, other classes, documentaries they have watched—anything is fair game. A third phase is to underline or circle what they believe is most relevant, thematic, or important. After writing, either put students in breakout groups to share what they've circled and underlined or ask a few individuals to share with the entire class.

INSTRUCTIONAL DESIGN BEST PRACTICES

An engaging course does not just happen. It requires careful planning using certain instructional design strategies to create a learner-centered course.

- Use Bulleted Lists - Transform large text blocks into visually appealing bulleted lists. Use custom fonts, graphics, and visual aids to make them even more powerful. Bold certain words or phrases that the student must remember. Remember to keep your lists simple. They should only contain essential information to avoid cognitive overwhelm. You can always add links for students to learn more about a certain item on the list.

- Add Creative Headers - While subheaders tell learners it's time to move on to the next subject, a header with a creative font or color helps set the tone for the subject you're about to discuss. For example, a red, bold header tells the learner to pay attention and conveys a sense of urgency.

- Provide Side Note Tips and Tricks - Instead of providing tips at the end of a lesson, provide special tips and tricks along the way. Side note hints provide better understanding and help clarify any confusion more quickly.

- Take Short Story Breaks - Storytelling gives online learners the chance to connect with the subject on a deeper level. Real-world examples put what they're learning into context and simplify the concept.

- Include Supplemental Resources - You can help online learners connect with your subject more fully by providing additional resources that allow them to learn more or explore the topic further.

- Highlight Important Quotes - Use creative fonts or pull quotes to emphasize key discussion points, facts, or figures that you want your learners to remember. Make sure you're selective about choosing them, as too many highlighted points can cause informational overload.

- Chunk Content - Break your topics into subtopics. Focus on one learning objective at a time and start another text block for every new idea.

- Use Scenarios - Much like storytelling, scenarios make the content come to life. They help learners go through a decision process and think more deeply. By making scenarios interactive, you engage and motivate learners. For example, if you are teaching a sales process, you could create a scenario of a salesperson trying to close a sale. This gives learners a chance to use the knowledge from the course

- Include Challenging Quizzes - You've probably seen the all too often true or false quiz used in online courses. These are not challenging. When using quizzes, it's important to vary the question type and use open-ended, multiple-choice, matching, etc. It's also important to pose challenging questions so that the learner's understanding is truly measured.

- Provide Quick Explanations and Feedback - By telling the learners why they are correct or incorrect, you motivate them to keep moving forward. Provide a brief explanation of the answer to reinforce the concept even further.

- Provide Rewards - People love receiving recognition after putting forth effort. It engages them and fosters a sense of achievement. Something as simple as a certificate after completing a course helps learners feel satisfied and motivated.

CHAPTER - 6

STRATEGIES FOR EFFECTIVE ONLINE COMMUNICATION

IMAGE IS EVERYTHING

Here are some dos and don'ts for choosing effective graphics:

Don't add graphics merely for decorative purposes. You may think it will draw attention, but it risks drawing attention away from what you're trying to teach. Images should serve a purpose and stay on topic.

Do use an illustration of a concept you are teaching. A representational image is a "realistic" depiction of a person, place, thing, or symbol. It does not need to be a photograph. For example, you could add a simplified line drawing of a bicycle.

Do use visual displays of relationships between things, such as pie charts or bar graphs.

Do use graphics that illustrate a process of transformation from one stage to another, such as in a flowchart, or progressive images.

Do use graphics to help explain an abstract concept. A cell molecule becomes easier to understand with an illustration.

Do opt for quality images over quantity. Poor resolution images lead to a poor perception of the quality of the course. If you can't find any suitable images, then it may be worthwhile to design your own or have one created for you.

INTRODUCING GAMIFICATION IN OUR TEACHING - ACTIVE LEARNING

PRESENTATION ON ACTIVE LEARNING

- What shields instructors from depending on dynamic learning all the more frequently?

- It takes more class time, so educators can't cover as much material in one class.

- Planning dynamic learning practices takes more prep work, which educators can't generally extra.

- Many educators have done well as instructors up to this point, so they are less disposed to redesign their present instructing techniques.

- Instructors come up short on the help, materials, and spending plan from their academic foundation to attempt new educating techniques.

- Large class sizes forestall the practical usage of numerous dynamic learning techniques.

The most widely recognized obstruction we get notification from educators is the mix of the last two reasons — issues with help and versatility. Educators need all the more showing colleagues, more space, or more spending plans to purchase materials for in-class exercises. Eventually, and shockingly, actualizing progressively dynamic learning can feel like an issue.

REEVALUATING HOW YOU SHOW INNOVATION

Here are a couple of different approaches to carry dynamic figuring out how to your group through innovation:

- Discussion Boards — Have students take what they realized in class or readings and proceed with the conversation on the web. Expect students to choose something they discovered intriguing in the material, do additional research, and compose a couple of passages about what else they have realized on the subject. Moreover, they expect students to react to what their companions have shared.

- Online Adaptive Tutorials or Virtual Labs — Use an eLearning stage, for example, Smart Sparrow, to construct an online instructional exercise or lab experience where students can work through a material or practice an aptitude as frequently as vital, at their own pace, time permitting.

- Virtual Field Trips—Several educators utilizing Smart Sparrow have made stunning "field trip" encounters that authorize students to investigate far off spots the world over from a first individual perspective. We've seen archeological burrow destinations, the Australian outback, and even their college grounds. Students can click around to become familiar with what they're seeing, answer addresses when provoked by their "control," and get customized criticism to their reactions.

GAMIFICATION: THE POWER OF LEARNING BY PLAYING

The main goal of teachers is how to motivate their pupils to learn because learning often depends on the composition of heterogeneous classes. These can include both capable students to activate effective learning strategies, use knowledge well already acquired, and do not be discouraged in the face of difficulties and both by students who, instead, they process the contents superficially, they don't have the strength to persisted in the face of obstacles and showed little confidence in their ability. In an educational context of pupils with these characteristics, teachers are inevitably faced with severe educational challenges. Challenging. It, moreover, puts in crisis the teaching scheme today more commonly used, based on sequence explanation, individual study, and written and oral verification. Through Gamification, we try to structure learning by examining a psychological construct of great interest and educational relevance, such as motivation to learn through play. Currently, there has been a rediscovery of the game as an activity considered severe. The games have recently aroused interest in the world related to training in the company, in management, and school, as a support to the processes cognitive and educational, and only recently, this interest has known an exceptional thrust and found appropriate practical formulations. The theme of the game and its use in educational contexts has today assumed the semblance of Gamification.

Responding appropriately is becoming increasingly important and indispensable. It is because an increasing number of organizations among the most advanced is introducing Gamification-based applications, both because the phenomenon has the potential to revolutionize in many ways the way you learn, you work, you communicate, and you do business. The inevitable consequence is an inflated use of the term, often a real abuse, which threatens to lead him to empty its intrinsic meaning gradually. That's why you want to start the journey inside the world of Gamification through answers to defined key concepts previously that will serve to clear doubts and misunderstandings about this phenomenon.

That the games have accompanied the history of man in the millennia is well known, and it is an intensely studied theme. Neuroscientific studies clarify that the practice of the game directly affects some primary human instincts, such as the need for self-expression or the willingness to pose new challenges, allowing to create engagement, motivation, and loyalty. Yet the cultural footprint which has always accompanied the playful phenomenon over time has severely limited its spread, relegating the game to niche practice or entertainment.

Gamification ' is a term not entirely transparent, partly controversial, understood with a variety of accents derived from game, so it has to do with the idea of play. Gamification can, therefore, be represented as a kind of "substrate," a level made of rules and strategies typical of the playful world (called " game mechanic "or" game technique") that we can superimpose and apply to other worlds, such as that of learning, training or marketing.

PREPARING FOR ONLINE TEACHING TRANSITION

Transiting into online teaching is much easier than you think. You don't necessarily have to be tech-savvy to be able to present your lectures online. Online education has been on the rise right before now. There have been several improvements in it, and thus, it is now easy to utilize. However, since you probably have not done it before now, you need to take your time to adjust to it. Online teaching is flexible, but for a newcomer, who is just taking the step into it, you may find it hard, and it may take a while for you to adapt to it. Fortunately, there are steps you can take that will help you transit easily and effectively into online teaching. Usually, there is a fear of ineffectiveness in many teachers. And this fear has often stopped or discouraged them from taking their classes online. But if you will take the following steps, then you will achieve an effect in your online teaching.

THE TRANSITION STEPS

Plan Your Classes

Online teaching is done with physically absent students. In most cases, you will not be available online at the same time for the lecture to start. Also, you need to understand that your students might be in different time zones, which doesn't tally with yours. Hence, you need to plan carefully to bridge these gaps. Online students have different needs from physical students. You need to plan your classes based on their needs. Create your syllabus and have every necessary material prepared. The students will easily know if the classes will fit in into their daily activities or not. Make them aware of any imminent quiz. Remember, they may be receiving your lectures in the middle of the night. Imagine what a surprised quiz will look like in such a situation. Hence, have every activity laid out and planned.

Understand Your Technology

Although you are not expected to be tech-savvy to start online teaching, you still need to have a good knowledge of the technology you are using for the classes. This involves your investing in the software and hardware that will be suitable for your planned classes. You should get a reliable computer. Your connection to the internet must be strong, and you should identify a suitable platform to organize your lectures. One such platform is Moodle. Make sure you research every tool you will be using so you can get the best.

Create a Suitable Working Environment

Since you are working remotely, you need to make sure that your environment is conducive to teaching. Remote works often become difficult without a good environment and self-discipline. You only need to set up your plans rightly. Set up a space that will work effectively for you to give your lectures.

Engaging in Innovative Discussions

The level of interaction in an online class is typically low. You must make sure that you set up an engaging and innovative environment. This will make your students want to stay. It will as well take away the coldness feature of online classes. Give room for your students to participate.

Create Communication Always

The life of online teaching is communication. You need to always be online. The first thing is to introduce yourself and give room for your students to introduce themselves as well. You need to bring in humanity into your class. Allow your students to always contact you if there is a need. Also, be available to provide answers to their questions as soon as they need it. This will increase their trust in you.

Create Motivation for Students

Learning is done differently by people. Motivation is the key to make sure that everyone learns despite their differences in learning methods. Not all students are self-motivated. You need to always motivate your students so they can gain from your classes. Your motivation may come in the form of giving extra points for contributing during the online discussion and for performing excellently in their assignments.

Seek Help and Feedback

Always ask for feedback from your students. They will provide you with valuable feedback that will help you improve your online teaching. Your students enjoy a more online presence than you. They are exposed to online tools that will help you provide better teaching. Seek their feedback, and you will receive the best responses that will be of aid to you from them.

Online teaching is an opportunity that you need to embrace as a teacher in this period of isolation and schools' closure. You can't afford to have your students staying home without lectures for as long as the virus is ravaging. Online teaching is flexible and will prevent your students from boredom once you approach them rightly and get them involved. The process of transiting is easier than it looks.

TIPS FOR AUDIO AND VIDEO

We must have elements of visual learning to create a quality online course. Adding video to your course is one of the most effective ways to engage students visually. This can be in the form of:

- Animations
- Talking head person
- PowerPoint slides with voice-over

- Slideshow

- Facebook Live

People often learn best when they connect with a human being - even if it's on screen. By choosing to appear on screen yourself, it allows you to personally engage with your audience. This is very effective for more classroom-based or theoretical type subjects.

There are many choices of video editing software that you can use:

- Camtasia - Widely used for all types of video with powerful editing features.

- Screenflow - One of the more popular screencasting and video editing tools.

- Adobe Captivate - Used by Instructional Designers, this is a true e-learning authoring tool, with a slightly steeper learning curve.

- Adobe Premiere Pro - A robust video editing tool. A bit more time consuming to learn.

- Movavi - Very affordable and very easy to use. Also, does screen capture recording with voice over.

- Vizia - A free tool that lets you add interactive quizzes, polls, response questions directly to a video.

There are also several free video editing software and screen recording tools available:

- FFSplit

- Cam Studio

- iSpring FreeCam

- Ezvid

- MadCap Mimic

- Flashback

- Fraps
- Screencast-O-Matic
- PicPick
- Bandicam

When creating a video, you'll also need to consider where you will host your videos. Widely used choices include YouTube, Vimeo, and Wistia.

HOW TO GET COMFORTABLE WITH BEING ON CAMERA

To appear on camera may seem intimidating, but it doesn't have to be. The voice in your head may be saying, "I look awful. I'm not attractive enough." This is simply not true. You bring your unique self to your course along with your own style.

It Doesn't Need to Be Perfect

Truth be told, most people are afraid of putting themselves on camera. It's normal. If you have these fears, they might keep you from starting. It's an obstacle that you'll need to overcome.

Once you bring your fears to the forefront of your mind, they instantly lose their power over you. The first step is to try it. You'll soon see that it's not so scary after all. It doesn't need to be perfect. People like to connect with a human. Your students will want to connect with you as a person.

Have Fun

A positive attitude is contagious. When you're happy, it's easy to transmit positive energy. When you smile, it makes other people smile.

When you're having fun, when you love sharing your story, people feel it. They're attracted to what you have to say because you make them feel good. They feel connected to you and are inspired to continue watching.

Everyone wants to learn from someone they like and trust. That's how you create genuine connections with students. When students love your teaching, they become students for life.

Practice on Camera

Don't wait until showtime to create your video. You don't want that kind of pressure. Even worse, you'll feel awkward and disappointed. It might also make you want to give up.

That's why it's best to practice ahead of time - as many times as you need to get comfortable in camera.

Start with a few quick and easy videos for fun. Send a birthday video message to a friend. Go on Facebook Live with a group of friends. Do a Skype call to someone far away? Keep doing this until you feel comfortable.

Once you put yourself in front of a camera several times, you'll get more accustomed to how it feels.

Practice Looking into The Camera

The next time you're on a Face Time or Skype call, look at the lens of the camera instead of the face of the person you are speaking to. Listen to how the person is reacting to you, but don't look at the actual person.

This will help you get comfortable speaking into the lens, without the visual clues of your audience. It might feel strange at first, but it works! Even though it doesn't feel like it, you'll be surprised to know that the person you are speaking to will feel like you're connecting.

Remember It's Not About You

Have you noticed when you speak with someone you know and like, you never think about what your hands are doing? You're simply engaged in the conversation, effortlessly connecting. Why? Because you're focused on the other person, and not on yourself. That's why speaking into the lens is important. It will feel strange at first, but when you focus on how you want your students to feel, you instantly take your attention off yourself.

This takes away the self-consciousness. When you're connected to the passion of your subject and your intention to help your students grow, your positive energy radiates from you effortlessly.

Prepare Your Words

While it may be tempting to "wing it," chances are you'll ramble on instead of delivering a confident and clear message. People have very short attention spans and will lose interest if you don't get to the point.

That's why you should make sure you map out exactly what you want to say in advance.

Whatever type of video you are creating, each video should have the following:

• Strong beginning - state what you intend to accomplish

• Two to three compelling ideas - this your main content

• Clear ending, or call to action - it should summarize and restate your intention

Dress for Success

We all feel better when we put a little extra effort into our appearance. What would you wear if you were teaching your students in person? Do you have a favorite shirt that makes you feel confident? Does your hair look better when you have it professionally styled? You'll want to look your best, so you can feel your best.

Add Interactive Features to Your Video

Interactive video helps your students learn more effectively and holds their attention longer. By asking questions at key points, you can highlight specific pieces of information that you want your students to remember. You can use a free tool called Vizia to add interactivity to your videos. Here are some ways to use it:

• Add periodic quizzes throughout your video, instead of at the end of the lesson.

• Add open-ended response questions to your video.

• Include a poll directly in the video to learn more about your students. It's a great way to conduct an immediate assessment of their skill levels, goals, and potential obstacles to learning.

• Create a promotional video with a quiz. You can show viewers the results of their quiz after they enter their email address. This can help you grow your email list before launching your course.

• For an effective call to action, add an external link directly on your video that takes them to a landing page, or any resources you mention in your video.

Use Audio Effectively

Good quality audio narration helps reduce cognitive overload, and it enhances the learner's interest. Make sure it's in a friendly, conversational tone.

CHAPTER - 7

USING MEDIA AND
TECHNOLOGY TOOLS

Online teaching has evolved over the years. People now stay in the comfort of their rooms to receive lectures. Technological innovations have made teaching easy. Everything that teachers need to get started is online. The incredible thing is the significant presence of people online. Millions of people are either browsing, reading, or surfing the internet every second. It makes it easier for you to gather your audience quickly. But before going further, let's look at what teaching is all about.

Teaching is the process of helping someone to acquire knowledge, competence, virtue. We have one thing or another that we can teach to people. These unique skills we have can help people. Some people desire to know the talent that you have.

Often, we find it difficult to under "what is teaching? Most people associate the word teaching and teachers with schooling or schools. But if I may ask, "Do you believe that teaching is only related to school? I think the best way to find the answer is to understand what teaching is all about.

Getting started with online teaching is the most challenging phase. It is the phase when you plan how to start your class. How to look for the audience and how to maximize profit.

Online teaching might sound difficult in the initial stage because you are not yet acquainted with it. You are just starting.

The rate of online education is increasing every day. More people are beginning to see the value of online learning.

Let's look at some ways to get prepared for your online teaching.

GETTING MATERIALS

Starting online school will require a lot of tools at the initial beginning. You would not like your students to get bored or encounter issues when they enroll in your course. You will need to get your necessary tools together. Most of the required tools that you will need include;

Computer and computer peripherals

A portable PC or laptop will help you to get started. With the PC, you can be able to create your course and upload it online without glitches. You don't need a supercomputer since you might not be running a high-level computer program. But I would advise that you get a PC that has a high resolution of at least 15 inches. With that, you can have full coverage. A broad coverage will benefit both you and your students. You can be able to do a live video with your students.

If you are using a Personal computer, you might need some computer peripheral's like keyboard, flash drive, mouse, speaker, etc. All those things depend on the course you are planning to teach.

Internet Access

This is one of the crucial things that you need. You will be spending a whole lot of your time online teaching your students or interacting with your students. An active internet connection will help you not to get frustrated.

Workstation

Remember that appearance creates a beautiful impression. So, you might invest a few dollars making the place look good and attractive. In other to understand better, see your work station as your office where you teach your students.

Software

You might not need much software to get started. You might only need office 365 like MS Word, Excel, PowerPoint, Outlook, and OneNote. But the type of software you need depends on the course you want to teach. If you're going to teach your students Architecture, you might need software like Autodesk AutoCAD, Revit, ArchiCAD, etc. It all depends on the course you want to teach. I suggest that you take your time and know the type of course that you want to teach your students.

Printer and Printer Papers

This is a mistake people make when starting online school. They think that they don't need printer or printer papers. But they are wrong. Even though all your assignments and exams might be submitted online, there might still be materials that you might want to print from your course work. I believe that you might want to keep a hard copy of your syllable for future purposes. You might even want to print your course work and give it to friends offline. So, look for a portable printer and buy it before getting started.

School Materials

You might need to get your necessary school materials like pen, board, and marker, drawing sheet, highlighters, binders, notebook paper, etc. You might need these materials for illustration when you are teaching. Most people might prefer to give examples on the board; that's why you might need the board. A portable board is ok.

Video Camera

You might believe that your PC camera is good enough. Yes, it is ok to a certain extent. But there are some situations where you might need to video yourself giving illustrations on the board. Your phone or laptop camera might not be good enough, but a digital video camera will do the magic for you.

These and many more are the essential things that you need to get started with your online school. There are other things that you might need depending on the course you want to teach your students.

Audio

You can lose your video signal and still communicate. Lose your audio, and the session is over. Because of this, we need to start by prioritizing audio. Mediocre audio quality is tolerable in short meetings, but first-rate audio becomes vital for longer and regular teaching sessions. The more energy our learners must exert to hear and understand what we are saying, the less energy they have at their disposal for the hard work of learning. Because only our students hear our voices, we can easily overlook audio quality. This is why it's so important to test our audio by recording and listening to a short segment.

Most devices come with an adequate microphone built into them. However, we won't know our sound quality until we test it. To check, log in to your videoconferencing software and play with the audio settings. In Zoom, you can access a test meeting room at https://zoom.us/test. In the audio settings, you can record a small segment and replay your audio. Record your voice and replay it a few times, giving attention to the volume, the way sound bounces off the walls of your space, and ambient noise or buzzing. Does your voice sound full and pleasant? Or does the microphone limit the range of your voice and make it feel distant or anemic? If you plan to teach this way often, you will want to purchase a quality microphone, one that picks up the full range of your voice, so that your audio is warm and full, giving your students a more pleasant experience.

With a desktop microphone, the volume and tonal change as we move around. It's important to place our microphone close to us and to keep it at the same distance from our mouth throughout the session. Closer proximity to the mic allows it to pick up the full range of our voice and gives our students a consistent experience.

Headsets and earbuds help to localize sound. Because earbud and headset microphones stay at a fixed distance from our mouth, the audio volume and quality remain the same. The drawback of a headset is that it makes you look like an air traffic controller. It may not seem like a big deal, but a headset puts the tech visually out front, and it's our goal to move the tech into the background.

Bluetooth earbuds are less conspicuous, and their noise-canceling features make a notable difference by eliminating background noise. Apple and Bose both make more expensive, high-quality Bluetooth earbuds, but there are some reliable and less-expensive options available. However, I've noticed that most Bluetooth earbuds, including Apple's AirPods Pro, can make the speaker sound like they are talking into a tin can.

After plugging in a USB microphone or connecting a Bluetooth device, you'll need to select it within audio settings. In the bottom left-hand corner of the Zoom window, you'll see a microphone icon. There is an up-arrow just to the right of the icon. Click on this to reveal the audio menu. Next, select the correct microphone from the list.

Your Backup Microphone

"Two is one, and one is none." That quote is from one of my broadcasting professors in college. It means you always need to think through your backup equipment. When for no discernible reason, your microphone isn't working, what will you use as your backup? Know how to switch back over to your built-in computer audio quickly. The key is being ready. Invest a few minutes getting used to the audio controls in Zoom, or your other videoconferencing software, by practicing the switch between different audio devices.

Your Camera

You will need an HD camera that you can position at eye level. Most of the time, a built-in laptop or desktop camera will suffice. From testing several external HD webcams, I've found that Logitech makes the best quality and most reliable product. They rest on the top of a monitor, and you can adjust them for the best angle. Most of these webcams contain built-in microphones, but the audio is usually mediocre. Because of this, I still recommend using one of the audio solutions recommended above.

Your camera's angle is a critical element, and its importance is too often overlooked. The camera angle and your posture will communicate an ongoing and tacit message to your students. Filmmakers will tell you that camera angles are their go-to tool for conveying their message, especially power dynamics—and power dynamics impact learning. Here is a quick overview of what different camera angles communicate:

- Camera positioned below eye-level: We are looking down onto our learners and inadvertently expressing dominance. It is also less than flattering because the shot features our neck and highlights our nostrils.

- Camera positioned above eye-level: We are looking up to our students. If you're short like me, perhaps you're accustomed to this. On camera, this can inadvertently communicate passivity and a lack of authority.

- Camera positioned from the side or at an irregular angle: This communicates that things are off-kilter, disorganized, or that we are inattentive and unaware.

- Camera positioned at eye-level: This communicates we are all on a level playing field and that things are stable.

Laptops require some creativity to get at eye-level. The best solution is an adjustable standing desk, the kind you can place on top of an existing workspace. Not only does this help us set the right camera angle, but it also allows us to alternate between sitting and standing. If you need a temporary solution, find a box or use a stack of books to raise your laptop to eye-level.

If you are using a phone or tablet, you'll need a way to keep your device stationary and stable. I don't recommend using mobile devices for videoconference teaching because they have some software limitations.

Your Monitor

For many of us, our main computer is a laptop, so we sacrifice screen size for portability. Monitor size becomes even more important when we have larger classes and need to accommodate more students on the screen. If, like me, you wear glasses, or just experience eye strain at work, then seriously consider acquiring a larger external monitor to care for your eyes. Additionally, with an external monitor, you can take advantage of the dual-screen features built into Zoom, like putting your presentation on one screen and your students on the second screen.

Student Equipment

Your course syllabus or classroom protocols should state that participation in the course requires a webcam, microphone, and reliable internet connection. Communicate this in a prominent place on your course site and your syllabus and repeat it in your course messaging. Beyond this, we have little control over what devices students may use to access our class. Some will use phones, and others will use laptops or tablets. The most important thing is that they know how to access your Zoom classroom with their particular device and to test it before class. If you can recommend one piece of equipment to your students that will make the most difference for everyone's experience, it is to ask them all to wear headsets or earbuds. These cut out ambient noise and make it possible to have an unmuted classroom, something I'll recommend in future chapters. If students have no other choice but to access the virtual classroom using public Wi-Fi, then headsets or earbuds are a necessity.

Check Your Sound First

Remember to always check your sound before recording. Everyone has recorded the perfect lecture at least once on mute. Keep the sound at the same level, so if you record at different times, the final recording has a consistent volume level. I prefer not to mess around with sound editing because it takes too much time away from focusing on the course content.

Do not sit dead center on camera unless you want your video to look like a hostage video. Sit to the side and take up about 2/3 of the screen. Be aware of the remaining third of your screen. Look up "the law of thirds" and photography to get a better idea of how to arrange a screen for video recording. It's all about hitting the lines and much more specific than my simple explanation here.

Keep your website clean and avoid a lot of useless icons or apps. Only provide the information that a student needs and use technology that allows you to upload materials as quickly as possible without a lot of fuss or editing.

PowerPoint Plugin Authoring Tools

The PowerPoint plugin authoring tools use PowerPoint as the authoring environment. However, in addition to all the bells and whistles that PowerPoint offers, these tools allow instructional designers to add interactivities and assessments. Since most people are familiar with PowerPoint, they find these tools easy to use. iSpring Suite is one example of a PowerPoint plugin tool and is one of the most popular rapid eLearning tools on the market. This tool is easy to use, and the learning curve is minimal. It also has a considerable compilation of eLearning assets. You can create interactive modules with iSpring's QuizMaker, video and audio editor, and conversation simulator.

E-Learning programs created using iSpring Suite automatically adapt to mobile devices, as necessary. There is no need for developers to manually configure complex interactive elements when iSpring is used to create online learning materials.

Desktop Authoring Tools

These tools offer more flexibility to eLearning designers, but at the same time, there is a learning curve. Some of the most popular desktop authoring tools are Adobe Captivate and Lectora.

Adobe Captivate

The latest version of Captivate introduced the smart positioning feature for the increased responsiveness of online learning modules. You can also add responsive motion effects to your page elements and preview them by simply hovering over the objects.

Captivate allows you to create various simulation modes labeled as See for demonstrations, Try for "hands-on" training, and Test for assessment. Among the other features of Captivate are geolocation, multilingual support, LMS preview, and diverse distribution possibilities.

Lectora

Lectora is a very powerful rapid eLearning tool by Trivantis. Because it can produce high-quality interactions and because there is a higher learning curve than with other tools, some people do not consider Lectora a rapid authoring tool. However, once you learn how to use it, you can begin developing high-level eLearning courses very quickly. Lectora comes with image, audio, and video editing tools.

Cloud-based Tools

Cloud-based tools are tools that eLearning developers can access over the internet via a secure hosted system. The main benefits of these tools are that they do not require IT configurations, special set-ups, or licenses. Many eLearning developers turn to these tools because they allow collaboration with colleagues and can be accessed anywhere. One example of a cloud-based authoring tool is CourseArc.

CourseArc

Ease of use and built-in features are this tool's best characteristics. It is 100% cloud-based, so there is no need to download anything or to use plugins. There are several templates and pre-set building blocks that make it easy for instructional designers to create eLearning materials without hiring expensive developers or graphic artists.

CourseArc allows you to embed videos from YouTube and Vimeo to enrich your content and provide more learning materials to your learners. It also allows you to add interactive features like drag and drop and inline quizzes for more interactivity.

Built-in analytics are incorporated into the design as well so that you can monitor performance and track progress. You can have dashboard stats as well as detailed reports on responses and scores from your learners. Another great thing about this tool is that it is not only compliant with industry standards, but also with provisions that support full accessibility for individuals with disabilities.

This tool comes with great support for high-quality instruction as well as responsive support services. This means that you will not be left hanging if you have concerns or need clarification on using CourseArc's features.

Articulate 360

Articulate 360 is a multi-toolkit that puts together a suite of nine tools to provide the most comprehensive solutions to eLearning design. It is comprised of Studio 360 as a PPT add-in, the standalone Storyline360, and the Rise web service for mobile-ready courses. Articulate 360 has an extensive asset library (over 1.5 million in total assets) composed of characters, icons, templates, photos, and videos. It also has live online training to walk designers through the various features of the program. Additionally, there is a project recheck application that allows you to "test" your design with subject matter experts before going live.

Other Tools to Consider

In addition to the eLearning Suite and rapid eLearning tools, other software programs do not belong in either of these categories, as they are not authoring tools. However, familiarizing yourself with these programs can be extremely advantageous for creating powerful eLearning content.

SnagIt

SnagIt is software from TechSmith. This screen-capturing tool allows instructional designers to create highly engaging images, presentation videos, tutorials, and training documents. SnagIt is especially useful for developing technical training.

Raptivity

This tool can be used on its own or in tandem with other authoring tools. It features customizable interactions, as well as device responsive frames. You can use Raptivity to create interactions in HTML5 and Flash formats, and either add them to your eLearning course or string them together to come up with learning modules. The tool offers multi-language support as well as expert support. Raptivity-created learning materials are SCORM-compliant.

SELECTING THE RIGHT TOOL

Before planning about the appropriate development tool, you should take the budget, learning curve, and content requirements into consideration. Even though one tool may be perfect for creating simulations, it may not work for software demonstrations. It is suggested that instructional designers add as many eLearning tools to their arsenal as possible and use each one based on the needs and requirements of each course they develop.

The following questions should help you pick the eLearning tools that best suit your needs:

What type of eLearning are you creating: synchronous or asynchronous?

Does your course have social learning components such as wikis or forums?

What type of media will your course have?

What is the level of interactivity in your course?

Do you need a specific output file format?

How much money can you spend on the authoring tool?

When it comes to deciding which eLearning tool to use, you need to take into consideration your eLearning and training objectives, learning curve, as well as your budget.

Additionally, you should always keep your learners in mind and consider their needs as you think about the features to look for in your eLearning tool.

CHAPTER - 8

BUILDING HUMAN CONNECTION

Making an effort to build relationships with students can mean the difference in your wellbeing and job satisfaction. It can mean the difference between loving what you do, being juiced about your work, and excited to go to school every day, or feeling overwhelmed, stressed, and that none of what you do matters. It can mean the biggest difference when things get tough.

Building positive relationships is the cornerstone of a teacher's work. When we create positive connections with students, we provide some motivation for them to learn and a safe space in which to learn. Student-teacher relationships are important because students need to feel safe enough to fail. They need an environment where it is accepted and expected that they will make mistakes.

A great online teacher is a good listener. Take the time to find out what students are interested in, what music they like, movies they watch, and the games they play. Use playground duty, school excursions, before and after school times to work on relationships with kids, and get to know them. Playing "get to know you" games during class time at the beginning of the year is another effective way to gather information about students and for students to get to know each other. Incorporate your students' interests to make the learning relevant, meaningful, and engaging. Give students a choice in their learning, showing that you value their input and perspective. Let them choose topics to study, even if it is only a choice between 2 possibilities. Give them opportunities to voice their concerns and their point of view about matters in the classroom and the school. Set up class meetings where students can discuss anything that is bothering them and come up with solutions to problems either with social or academic issues.

ALLOW STUDENTS TO GET TO KNOW YOU

People like to connect with a human. Consider including a video introduction of yourself.

While you want to appear professional, show that you have other interests or a sense of humor. Don't be afraid to add some personality to your profile. This will help students to feel more comfortable communicating with you and will set a tone for an open environment.

Include a quality photograph of yourself

Make sure your bio picture clearly shows your face. You want students to be able to put a face with a name. Is it conveying the message that you want to be conveyed? Does it look friendly? Approachable?

Open the door to conversation

Invite them to answer a question in the discussion area. Ask: "Where are you from?" and "Why did you decide to take this course?" This opens a conversation, and it helps you confirm the relevant aspects of your course. Make sure you let them know how long it takes for you to respond to any questions. While other students may provide answers, students will be looking for your response as confirmation. The more conversation, the more the relationship will grow.

Create a social media group

Create a Facebook group and host a Facebook live session

Student insights can pop up all over a site by quoting them. You can quote student comments in a video lecture. Sometime in the announcements, I'll suggest students read certain classmates' posts.

COMMENTS IN SPEED GRADER

The best feature in Canvas is something the company calls "Speed Grader," and it carries a little trademark sign, so I think the company is aware of how efficient it is.

It allows instructors to write comments back to students and attach Word Documents if you, like me, use the track changes and the comments feature in Word to give feedback.

In the grading message box, use the student's name. Don't just give a copy and paste feedback that you send to each student. Assume some students know one another and will share what feedback they receive.

USE REPLIES ON THE DISCUSSION BOARD POSTS AS A "HIDDEN LECTURE"

Use students' names when replying and comment on their writing style if it's relevant. Perhaps there is a phrase or word that deserves mentioning. Any feedback is helpful.

Vague answers that do not cite evidence from the text get zero points. Students quickly learn that my discussion boards are not a one-sentence busy-work assignment. The more substantive the initial post, the more substantive the classmate replies will be. On course evaluations, my students observe that my discussion boards "feel" like an in-person one. They also say that this kind of discussion does not happen in other online courses. What is everyone else doing? I don't know. But here's another point: students will work hard if the instructor works hard. Don't phone it in and then expect the students to do everything.

DEVELOP FORMAL ASSIGNMENTS OUT OF DISCUSSION BOARD POSTS

Let the discussions lead you to the formal paper prompts. One time a student post gave me an idea for a paper prompt, so I quoted the student in the prompt. It's a way for the class to feel connected.

Don't miss an opportunity to connect with students. If they send you an email, then use it as a chance to break through the distance and say something about their progress in the course. Repeating or noticing a person's language is a great way to make them feel seen and heard. Online learning gives instructors plenty of material to work with.

CHAPTER - 9

BUILDING COMMUNITY

GROUP WORK

Check how your learning management system uses Groups setting. In Canvas, under the "People" tab on the navigation panel on the left-hand side of the screen, you'll find the controls for creating groups.

First, decide if you wish to create groups, let the Canvas assign students, or let students self-select.

Be Careful When Setting up Group Discussions

To have the Groups work, then you have to select "Group Project" in the Discussion Board settings. If you forget and the students post to the board, then you cannot undo the discussion board and create a group one.

If you use Group settings, then students will only have access to work form group members.

BUILDING A COMMUNITY ONLINE

It is where the bulk of the work lies. It is where you employ your marketing strategies. Now that you have finished setting up your website, it is now time to find students that will enroll in your online class. The best way to build an online community is by identifying your target audience. Once you identify your audience, it is now time to reach out to them.

There are so many ways that you can reach out to your audience online. These tips will help you to find students to get started with your online school. If you have already started, most of these tips will also help you to increase your online community. Let's look at these tips one by one;

Social Media

It is one of the best ways of reaching out to your audience. There are many social media platforms that you can utilize to promote your school like; Facebook, Twitter, Instagram. When running campaigns, focus on what the students will gain from your course. Use explainer videos to run social media campaigns. Videos tend to draw the attention of people quickly than written text.

If you have already started your online school, social media is also another avenue to boost your online community. Social media will allow you to reach out to parents, families who would want their wards to enroll in an online class.

Website Optimization

A responsive website will create a good impression. Let your website create a good impression in the mind of your visitors. If students visit your site, and they find it challenging to navigate to various pages, they won't spend time on your website, and they will leave unsatisfied. Optimize your website in a way that it would be easy to navigate. Increase your site loading speed and let your website have clear policies. State your goals and objectives clearly on your website so that visitors will know what they stand to gain from your course. Optimize your website from the theme, pages, policies, and the login page. Make everything to be simple and clear.

Improve Your Organic Search

Even though you will be running loads of social media campaigns, do not overlook the power of google search engine. There are millions of people worldwide conducting an online search on your course. Until they stumble on your course online, they won't enroll. That is, while attracting search engine presence is very crucial in building an online community. If you already have your school online, work on your search engine.

Leverage on the power of Google AdWords

That's another way of reaching out to parents and students online. It will allow you to reach out to parents the very moment they are researching. Planning successful online advertising will help to increase your online presence quickly.

However, before you can have a successful online advertising campaign, you need an adequate understanding of how those platforms work. Here are just a few tips that would help you to run a successful campaign;

- Write a compelling Ad copy using your keywords. Let your Ad copy encourage students and parents to click on your Ad.

- Create a unique landing page. Build a landing page that discusses your objectives. Your landing page should be very responsive.

- Send your visitors directly to your landing page. That will make them see what they are looking for quickly.

- Understand what parents and students are looking for and deliver it on your page. You can do keyword research or spy your competitors to know what students and parents are looking for online.

- Monitor your advertising campaign from time to time. It will enable you to know where your traffic is coming from and your ROI. One way of doing that is by integrating google analytics to your platform.

Use your Offline Contacts to leverage on your Online Activity

Even though you are running online campaigns, you can also leverage your offline connections. You can reach out to friends and family. You can create posters and billboards. You can communicate with parents and students offline. Talk to them about your online school.

Webinar and Podcast

That's is another avenue to reach out to friends. You can host live webinars where you talk about your school. You can also send out a prerecorded podcast to your friends online. These are ways of reaching out to people easily and quickly online.

Increase Your Online Presence

Boost your online presence across various social media platforms. Let's assume that you have 4000 Facebook friends. When you post your advert in your timeline, it will likely reach out to at least 25 percent of your friends, which is 1000 friends. Let's say you still have such a fan base across other social media platforms; you will be reaching thousands of people daily without running any campaign.

There are different ways you can use to promote your online school like;

Hosting offline seminar: Where you gather people and talk about your school.

Media campaign: You can run a television advert, radio advert, press release. These avenues will avail you the opportunity to reach out to millions of students and parents.

Note: Always state your objectives clearly in your campaigns to avoid issues in the long run. Let's move over to the final part of this section, which talks about pricing.

CHAPTER - 10

GIVING FEEDBACK AND TIPS TO MAKE IT HAPPEN

Technically, feedback is the return information or, if you want to be more precise, the process by which the effect is resulting from the action of a system (mechanism, circuit, organism, etc.) is reflected on the system itself to vary or correct its functioning properly. In our case, during the lesson, especially during an explanation, it is important to ask students if they understand if we were clear if it is necessary to repeat a concept, information, etc. With the feedback technique, on the one hand, we make sure that all students are up to date with the explanation, but, from the relationship, we are telling students that we are interested in their learning. Again, our nonverbal communication must be as positive as our intentions.

If you're a perfectionist, you might not like this next statement: In an online class, prompt feedback is more important than quality feedback.

That's not to say that you can't have both; but, if you are like me, you're familiar with how it goes: sometimes you just don't have that two-hour block of time to focus on grading. During such times, our tendency (at least my tendency) is to put it off until tomorrow. Most of the time, this isn't procrastination; it's just that we want to deliver substantial feedback to our students, and we hope tomorrow will offer us that uninterrupted chunk of time we need. Oftentimes, tomorrow turns into three days, and three days turn into a week, and...

By the time we engage our students, they're on to the next week's reading, a new discussion, or some other assignment. Because of this, we need to strike while the iron is hot, while what they have learned is still fresh in their minds.

FIVE PRACTICES FOR DELIVERING PROMPT FEEDBACK

Draw a Line in the Sand

By setting a date, we prevent ourselves from pushing out our response time in the hope of that uninterrupted space for grading. Decide on how far out is too far out for replying to discussions, or for sending feedback on a particular assignment. Of course, these timeframes will differ based on the nature of the assignment.

Set a Regular Time

Residential courses have a set time for class, so why not schedule regular, weekly times for grading, commenting, and responding to emails?

Use Tools for Rapid Return

Some technologies are complex and slow down the feedback process; others speed it up. It all depends on the nature of the assignment and on what works best for you. Are paper and pen your preferred method of grading? If so, let your technical support team know. Your school may have a scanning option for you to use

Use Rubrics to Simplify Grading

Rubrics take some of the subjectivity out of grading. If a student gets a 7 out of 10 on a discussion grade, you don't have to write a paragraph describing why they earned that grade; you can simply refer them to the rubric descriptors. This is where that comment box does come in handy when grading discussions.

CHAPTER - 11

STRATEGIES FOR

FORMATIVE FEEDBACK

You'll remember this feeling from your years as a student: after spending a week or two slaving over an important paper, you finally turn it into your professor. Then the day comes to get your paperback. You did okay; maybe not as well as you had hoped, but you knew your professor had high expectations. So, you begin flipping through your paper to read the comments. Page one—nothing. Page two—a brief comment about your punctuation. Pages three, four, five, six—nothing. Page seven—something indiscernible, but it appears to be about one of your citations. Your next paper is due in a week, and you're left with little idea for ways to improve.

Student course evaluations are full of versions of these two statements:

1. "I would have liked our professor to interact with us more."

2. "I had hoped for more feedback on my assignments."

They want interaction, a sense of connection. They also want to know what you think about their work and how they can improve. Even the best courses with the best instructors still see these requests for more interaction and feedback.

SUMMATIVE VS. FORMATIVE FEEDBACK

Summative feedback focuses on assessment; it comes after the student completes and submits the assignment. It's performance-driven and usually involves giving your students a grade. The benefit of summative feedback is that it gives you and the learner a way to measure their learning. For example, let's say you have assigned an essay. You receive all the papers on the due date, mark a grade, leave comments, then students read the returned papers.

Formative feedback is more of dialogue; at least it creates space for conversation. Formative feedback focuses on the process of learning, so students receive feedback while they are crafting their assignments. Formative feedback is less assessment-focused and more learner-focused, engaging the student where they most need to build understanding and skill. Instead of simply assigning an essay, you might implement a peer review where students share their essays and work through a common evaluation rubric. You could participate in these as well, evaluating and commenting on their drafts. Then your students could submit their revised papers for a final grade. You should get better papers, and we all know that better papers are easier to grade.

As an educator, you can see the benefits of taking a more formative approach with your students. There are three ways you can use formative feedback in your online course.

Invitation to Dialogue

Students find the online environment new and disorienting. When they had a question in their face-to-face class, they simply raised their hand or talked with you about their paper after class. In-person, this just kind of happened. In the online environment, you'll have to create spaces for formative feedback and conversation. Unfortunately, most instructors don't pursue their students in this manner. They expect that their students will contact them with questions. Remember, your students are disoriented, and they need some cues. Also, they are probably not used to taking such an active role in the course. So, you'll have to invite them to interact (and you'll have to make that same invitation several times). For K-12 students, I'd even recommend creating a communication/dialogue grade for each quarter.

A few ways to do this:

During those busy weeks when you know your students are working on a major project, send out an email to let them know you're available to help them. End your email with, "Simply reply to this email if you have any questions."

If you have certain office hours and are open to taking phone calls, let them know when you are available that week. Be sure to post your phone number on the course site or in the email.

If you receive a particularly good question from a student, post it as a course-wide email or put it in an Assignment FAQ page.

Whatever strategies you choose, the key is to invite them multiple times, especially at the beginning of the semester. This can help create a culture of dialogue in your course and has significant payoff during the second half of the semester.

Set up an All Class Paper Discussion Forum

In this discussion forum, students post their questions about the assignment. They might need help finding credible sources, or it could be that they are having a difficult time understanding a particular concept. If your course site uses groups, I'd recommend turning group mode off for this discussion; that way, everyone in the course can see and reply to all the questions that students post. Most discussion boards allow you to subscribe; this way, you get an email alert whenever a student posts a new question. Now, this can get overwhelming and is unnecessary for most discussions, but this forum won't get hundreds of posts like regular discussions. Instead, it becomes a dynamic FAQ page, with most students reading the responses to the questions they would have asked. Sometimes you'll find that you don't need to reply because another student has already beaten you to it. Because of this, assignment discussion forums can generate meaningful student-to-student interaction.

This can be a real timesaving strategy. If a student emails you with a question that you've already answered in the Paper Discussion forum, you don't have to retype the whole thing; simply send them to the forum. It also gives you a ton of valuable feedback. When you go to redesign or just improve your assignments, the assignment discussion forum will provide you with more helpful and targeted feedback than your course evaluations.

A Quick Tip: To prevent any confusion, it's important to set up separate discussion forums for different assignments.

Ask Students for the Feedback They Need

I'll admit that this is more of a summative strategy, but it's one of my favorites because it's a formative take on summative feedback. Ask your students to type a few questions on the final page of their paper. Their questions may range from confusion about citations, questions on composition, to wondering if their ideas about the subject matter are on track. This gives you a place to start when grading, and it helps you to tailor your feedback to your student's needs. This moves your students into a reflective mode, where they are considering their learning and requirements. Additionally, it casts your feedback as a conversation.

Another Quick Tip: To get this to work, you'll probably need to require a certain number of questions from your students, and for those questions to be part of their paper grade.

If you're relatively new to teaching online, then I'd recommend just picking one of three practices and trying it out this semester. And if you had to pick just one, pick #1, Invitation to Dialogue.

CHAPTER - 12

DEALING WITH

DIFFICULT STUDENTS

CRITICAL WEEKS FOR ENGAGING THE BOTTOM 20% OF LEARNERS

An after-school remedial reading program in Ohio decided to only accept first graders. Why? All the research pointed to first grade as the most critical year for developing literacy. If students fell behind in the first grade, they would likely never catch up.

Similarly, weeks three and four of an online course have strategic significance. At this point, you now have a few weeks of data on your students-enough to see patterns in their participation. Somewhere between 10-20% of students in an online course will show patterns of absence or disengagement. If this pattern is not addressed early in the course, these students are likely to remain detached the entire semester and become Emergency Students. You know them all too well because they end up creating more work for you, especially at the end of the semester. But there is a magic bullet for this.

What these students need is a bit of immediacy, an email from you letting them know that you are aware of their lack of participation in the course.

When students become aware that they can see their site activity and their lack of engagement, they usually will rally and take a new approach to the course. As well, contacting a student sometimes surfaces other issues-a technical problem, some larger family problem, or an illness—allowing you to connect with the student and to connect them with other school resources: Dean's office, Guidance Counselor, etc.

To gather this information means some technical work on your part. Almost all learning management systems (Moodle, Blackboard, etc.) have reporting features. Browse around on your course administration section and get familiar with these. Lean on your institution's technical support team if you need some help.

What you're looking for:

- Students who have not logged into the course site as often

- Patterns of not submitting course assignments - Patterns of not accessing critical course media - Low grades on submitted work

What's Next?

After you've identified the 10-20% of students who are struggling or just disengaged, send them an email. Instead of writing up a new email for each student, you can use this template when you contact them.

AN INOCULATION AGAINST ABSENTEEISM?

The best long-term solution for online absenteeism is your consistent presence in the course. In general, the courses with the lowest student absenteeism are the courses where teachers are the most present.

CHAPTER - 13

FOSTERING STUDENT PERSISTENCE AND SUCCESS

RECIPE FOR A GREAT ONLINE CLASSROOM SESSION: WHAT STUDENTS SAY WORKS

The following seven student recommendations are transferrable across both on-campus and on-Zoom classrooms. However, I propose that students experience the benefits of these practices at a higher level in this virtual space.

Create a Participative Environment

A fruitful academic discussion means hearing from everyone, or nearly everyone in the class. In large classes, allowing every student to speak can be difficult or downright impossible. But there are more ways to hear from someone than just giving them the microphone. Polls tell you what everyone is thinking, and breakout groups offer students to hear from everyone in their group.

Foster Group Stability

When given a choice between group variety and consistency of group membership, students favor consistency. Maintaining group membership allows students to develop a team culture, agreed-upon expectations, and it creates that sense of trust and safety needed for more demanding academic discussions and collaborations.

Practice Directive Leadership

At the beginning of a movie, film directors use an establishing shot to help the audience find their bearings. Typically, these are wide-angle shots that answer the questions, "Where am I?" and "What is going on?" Our students need the same kind of framing in the Zoom classroom. Clear classroom protocols and expectations

Assertive communication skills

The skills set needed to facilitate groups

Structuring sessions and creating class rhythms

Providing preparatory exercises and discussion guides

Be Curious

Students want a teacher who is both an expert and a fellow learner. They hope that we will know a lot without being a know-it-all. More than the subject matter, they want teachers who are curious about them and their learning process. This means we create space for emergent questions, and we strike a balance between pre-scripted elements and the freedom to go off-script. Students say such classes feel more "organic," and teachers report a higher sense of satisfaction when they feel grounded in a structure and remain open to serendipity. Curiosity makes this possible.

Tell Me Something New

Students who come prepared to class are ready for something new. The easiest way to stifle this yearning is to rehash material they have read or viewed. While this may seem an obvious thing to avoid, the rehash is a persistent practice to which both novice and veteran teachers fall prey. How might we move our students beyond information and into critical thinking? And into the realm of original ideas? These are the types of questions we'll address in the upcoming chapters on teaching and designing learning sessions.

Develop Quality Prompts

The quality of our learning conversations depends on the quality of the questions we ask. Students tell us they want to be challenged by questions and prompt that press to consider new perspectives and ways of thinking.

Make Course Materials Accessible

Our learners need access to the materials we use in class: presentations, files, articles, links, etc. We can provide these within a well-organized LMS course site or send them via email before class. Alternatively, we can prepare a simple text document so that we can quickly copy and paste links, questions, etc., into the chat window.

Design Meaningful Learning Tasks

Busywork is death to learning. We've all been subjected to it, and we've probably all been guilty of creating it. Busywork is usually the result of a well-intentioned learning activity gone awry, one that may only need a strategic tweak and integration into the life of the course.

With these learner-centered and learning-centered principles in mind, we now move to the second major element in our recipe for success: our classroom protocols. These guidelines have the power to eliminate distractions, create a safe learning environment, and set a positive culture where teachers can invest more time in learning and less time in classroom management.

BUILD HIGHWAYS FOR STUDENT SUCCESS

You could spend a ton of time perfecting your zoom face-to-face lectures to be delivered online, but do not do this, the payoff isn't worth it.

You could spend a ton of time recording and editing and rerecording and reediting your lectures to be delivered as videos, but do not do this, the payoff isn't worth it.

You could spend a ton of time revising your assignments so that students can do them on their own better, but do not do this, the payoff isn't worth it.

You could spend a ton of time individually emailing and soothing your students so that they feel better, but do not do this, the payoff isn't worth it.

Instead, spend your limited time available for teaching you building extremely clear "what to do today" pathways for your students to follow that, if they do them, they will nearly be guaranteed success.

CHAPTER - 14

MOTIVATING ONLINE STUDENTS

ALLOW STUDENTS TO CUSTOMIZE THEIR OWN LEARNING

Some students like to complete tasks in a perfectly sequential order. Other students may prefer to scroll through all of the lesson titles and complete them out of order, based on what seems most applicable to them. When you provide a bird's eye view of the skills and knowledge you'll cover, learners have the opportunity to adapt your course to their needs and desires. Some students may wish to move ahead through different lessons in the course, while others will prefer to stay within its sequential order. This will provide a better learning experience for all types of students by keeping them engaged and preventing frustration.

CONNECT TO HUMAN EMOTION

Most people remember information when it's tied to some form of emotion. It facilitates a passion for the subject and helps move people to action. Studies show that retention increases when courses appeal to emotion. That means that students are more likely to complete your course and give you a five-star review.

Without story and experience, your message will fall flat and leave students feeling disengaged from the information.

Here are some tips to help connect your students through emotion:

• Rather than emphasizing only skills and knowledge, make sure some of your learning outcomes focus on how your students will feel after completing your course.

• Your course description should explain how it will improve the lives of your students.

• Utilize emotion-packed words throughout your training course. Include the word "feel."

• Appeal to the higher meaning and purpose your target audience may have.

• Provide relevant examples and case studies of real people and events. Make sure you connect it to the subject you're teaching.

• Include reflective activities such as journal reflections and discussions in group forums.

PROVIDE OPPORTUNITIES FOR SELF-ASSESSMENT AND REFLECTION

When students can draw upon their own experiences to go through a personal learning process, they can apply new knowledge to their own lives in a meaningful way. It also provides another way to access emotion within your course. You can accomplish this through a variety of exercises and activities that encourage students to assess their own approaches to situations.

Here are some ideas on how to facilitate self-assessment in your course:

· Provide prompts for journaling and reviewing their journal entries.

· Include discussion opportunities within your course.

· Students could present a problem they had in the past and provide a summary of how they solved the problem. Have them explain the struggles they encountered, the emotions they experienced, and the strategies they used to overcome them.

· Create a questionnaire that causes students to personally reflect on specific topics in your course. For example, you could ask students how their thinking process has changed as a result of the course concepts.

· Create an action plan worksheet that encourages students to create their own plan for their progress in this subject area.

PROVIDE FAMILIAR ANALOGIES

By referencing concepts that are familiar to your students, you provide a way for them to connect to the subject in a way that has meaning to them. The language you use and the activities you include must be in a context they can relate to. This also helps you address the differences between individuals and find common ground. It means that you may adapt the way you present a certain topic to the needs of a particular audience. You might choose to capitalize on an interest such as football, where you would make a football analogy to describe the concept you're teaching. By adding some personal relevance to something outside of the course, it can engage students in the subject in a new way. This works particularly well when teaching complex subjects.

TIPS AND TRICKS TO MOTIVATE STUDENTS TO TAKE LESSONS

Inspiration is, in all actuality, one of the basic mainstays of a fruitful classroom. As a mentor, you won't achieve your objective without moving your understudies. Inspiration is certifiably not an entangled idea, and it's anything but a troublesome activity to spur the understudies. We live our lives with satisfaction and joy, with torment and distress, since we are motivated to push ahead. Better believe it, regularly being disregarded and dispirited in our lives, we keep away from our expectation of pushing ahead, yet when human instinct is empowered, we begin to reconsider pushing ahead. Similarly, as a rule, without being enlivened, the understudy loses would like to learn. That is the reason understudies should be propelled.

An educator can't be a decent instructor, except if he realizes how to move a student. An astounding teacher is an individual who knows the realities and strategies of how to make a functioning classroom, where the understudy can partake excitedly. As a general rule, without inspiring your understudies, you won't have the option to satisfy your sole duty.

There is an assortment of ways to deal with rouse understudies in the homeroom. Probably the best thoughts for empowering the understudies in the school are talked about underneath. As a general rule, these tips on persuading your understudies can assist you in making your classroom progressively beneficial and innovative.

Guarantee Anxiety-Free Classroom

What do you know? Dread additionally represses learning results. Along these lines, never try to force fear by authorizing disciplines in your classroom. Negative comments regularly offer ascent to fear among understudies in the classroom. The dread in the classroom, regardless of whether it's for revenge or compromising remarks, will never motivate the students. In all actuality, dread is a hindrance to taking an interest effectively in the learning meeting. The understudy ought to never look to take a functioning part in the classroom. That is the reason each educator ought to keep up a dread free class to rouse the understudies. Along these lines, they never offer negative expressions and troubling errands as disciplines.

Promote Their Ideas and Decisions

To advance imaginative learning in the homeroom. When offering assignments and coursework, give them their opportunity to pick the subject on their own. Your understudies will be motivated. You know, all things considered that individuals need appreciation. Truly, thankfulness changes a great number of understudies 'lives. Your understudies can't hold on to partake in your next talk. What's more, if you appreciate new thoughts, several incredible thoughts will likewise be presented to different understudies in your homeroom. So consistently welcome new plans to motivate your understudies.

Explain the Objective

Each understudy enjoys clear guidelines. Explain every objective and target objective to be cultivated toward the start of the course. Remember to refer to the impediments they may look during the meeting. Examine potential cures about the difficulties they may confront. They will, subsequently, be propelled to address more issues, which will make the subject progressively available. Accordingly, you will find that your homeroom has become fruitful because your understudies are empowered.

Improve the Environment of the Classroom

Don't generally plunk down to talk about the exercise. Move next to the students and consider the experience. Keep them out of your group once in a while. Instruct them to visit the library now and again for investigation purposes. The move in the classroom condition animates the energy of the learning cerebrum, which is, truth be told, an essential for inspiration.

Be a Good Listener

Listen cautiously to what your understudy needs to state. Value their feelings and conclusions. Find a way to take care of the issues they talk about. Be an incredible audience, fellow. They will adore you when you hear them out with legitimate consideration. You will win their certainty, hence. Presently, is it difficult to move them? On the off chance that you need your understudies to hear you out, you need to hear them out first.

Share Their Experience

Not all understudies can share their involvement with the course of the class. Some of them will be involved by understanding books. However, as sure understudies examine their exercises related mastery, others might be motivated to take an interest effectively.

Set up the exercise in such a rousing way, that different kinds of students can connect effectively in the sharing of exercises. In this circumstance, different understudies are regularly propelled to share their own encounters. You can, subsequently, guarantee that the classroom is effective.

Positive Competition

The helpful rivalry is, fundamentally, a valuable system in the school. Guarantee the contention is productive. A decent contention in bunch work propels students hugely. We are additionally arranged to complete network work, which will likewise carry noteworthy advantages to their expert life. There is no uncertainty that sound rivalry sparkles energy among the understudies in the classroom.

Know your Student Well

You have to realize your understudies well. You ought to likewise know their inclinations, their aversions, their viability, and their absence of execution. At the point when your understudies understand that you realize them well, they will start to like you and reveal their hindrances. This would be simpler for you to motivate your understudies correctly. You won't have the option to energize them since you realize them well.

Support Them and Give Them Responsibility

Give them the respect of the understudies. Allot them a class venture. They will work with assurance and without self-doubt. In such a circumstance, singular understudies may likewise need to satisfy their commitments. At the point when you give them obligations, trust inside themselves will develop, and they will start to feel that they are significant because they get an incentive from you. They would then be propelled to connect more in the classroom. At the point when you confide in them, they will consistently confide in you consequently.

Show Your Enthusiasm

To convey your excitement in the classroom during a talk while meeting your obligations. Offer your energy about their extraordinary achievement. Once more, it shows an idealistic premium when each student presents another thought. Your demeanor of excitement will empower them.

Hold Your Record

Compose a report for you. Record each achievement of your understudy. On the off chance that you locate that a particular understudy is changing, address the understudy about change. Show the understudy the record. Rewards and bolster the understudy before the classroom. Indeed, even offer the progressions with your companions. On the off chance that an understudy finds that you're dealing with the understudy while you address from your record, the understudy is enlivened.

Valuable Feedback

On the off chance that an understudy isn't progressing nicely, incorporate positive input. At the point when important, offer another opportunity. Be a companion and look to comprehend the instance of such an awful outcome. Urge the understudy to rouse him or her to improve rapidly next time as he or she didn't see how to do well in this subject with legitimate information and procedure. Alright, guess what? Your valuable surveys will change a great number of lives. Take a gander best case scenario understudies in your school; you will get a lot of good characteristics. Advise them regarding the delightful conditions they have. As a general rule, esteem them, which will rouse them altogether consequently.

Real-life Situation In the classroom

Relate your exercise plan to a genuine situation. Make the exercise charming with the fun of the game. Reveal to them an astounding story with a blend of amusingness. The perusing along these lines makes it feasible for the understudy to react to their understanding. Let them likewise apply the exercise to their understanding. Just track it precisely. In actuality, when you're managing your perusing, in actuality, situations, understudies are urged to learn and go to your group.

Communicate with Your Parents and Guardians

Utilize the homeroom to keep the guardians and gatekeepers on the up and up. You should welcome guardians to pursue an ordinary or week by week email overview of what's happening in their kids' schools. Messages contain the pending or incomplete work of an understudy, just as updates and questions that you post in the class stream.

Allotting Assignments to a Group of Students

Instructors may designate work and post-declarations to singular understudies or a gathering of understudies in a class. This usefulness encourages instructors to recognize guidance as required, just as to advance community-oriented gathering work.

Utilizing the Classroom Mobile App Annotations

Understudies and instructors can utilize the Mobile Classroom on Android, iOS, and Chrome cell phones. You can give a contribution to constant by explaining the understudy's work in the application. Understudies may likewise record their assignments to pass on a thought or idea all the more without any problem.

An educator must guarantee that the classroom is dynamic. Educators ought not to say that they can simply enter and leave the homeroom with 'Great Stories' without giving an effective class. Through rousing your understudies, you can make the best classroom you're anticipating. All things considered, just like an educator, you are setting up a nation, another world that will, before long, principle you and the planet.

CHAPTER - 15

CREATING AUTONOMY

HOW TO COMMUNICATE WITH YOUR STUDENTS

Communication is very crucial in online teaching. Speaking effectively is one of the problems that online tutors face. Often, we create a beautiful course that is captivating and attractive, but teaching the course is a big issue.

Communicate Respectfully

Take note of this when communicating with your students. Respect is the pillar for every effective communication, especially when it has to do with students. While sitting on the computer, it is easier to forget that there are students on the other side. Sometimes, students might ask you provoking questions. You might be pushed to reply to the student in a thought-provoking manner. But it is wrong. Always pause and meditate before you lash out to the student. Avoid character attacks or unnecessary accusations. If you disagree with your student on particular issues. Look for a way to address what he is saying rather than attacking the student.

While teaching, most notably during live videos, you will encounter a situation where the student is not paying attention. Sometimes, you encounter a situation where the student will ask you questions that you have said over and over again. It is left for you, calm down and address the situation. Like I said earlier, think about it that you are teaching your students offline. It will help you to handle some issues.

Below is a summary of ways you can demonstrate respectful communication:

Make use of a tone that is courteous and honest

That is, choose words that are appropriate to the situation. Avoid using inflammatory words. That is words that can infuriate the students or cause an emotional response.

Focus on what you are teaching

Avoid things that can distract you when you are teaching your students online. Sometimes, you see teachers walking out of the camera to attend to some needs and returning later. Most of those actions can infuriate the students. So, once you walk into your camera, focus on what you want to teach.

Apologize for your mistakes

Learn to apologize when you make a mistake. Some emergency might come up, and you will have to end the class abruptly. Apologize for ending the class and give the students tangible reasons while you need to end the class. It is very disrespectful, ending a live class without giving reasons.

Use clear and concise words

When you are communicating with your students, be clear as much as possible. It will help your students to understand you very well. Before you say something, give thought to what you want to say. Think about how your students will respond to such questions. Don't confuse your students with unclear sentences. If the topic is tough, look for a way to divide it into parts. In that way, your students won't struggle to understand it. Remember that they will only continue to enroll in a course that they are understanding. If your students do not understand what you are teaching, the majority of them will quit. Be brief when you are teaching. Avoid unnecessary words that are so irrelevant.

Make your communication personal

What do I mean? What I mean is making your communication feel real with the students. Make your students feel your presence. Communicate with your students in a way that they know you feel that they are real people and that you respect and value your communication with them.

One of the significant ways you can do that is by having a class discussion from time to time. In the class discussion, every student will be availed of the opportunity to interact with each other. It will boost the confidence of the students.

Start and End with Key points

In other to ensure that your students will understand your lesson, reiterate critical points at the start and end of the course. Another way to do that is by adding a footnote at the end of the course. The note will serve as a reminder to the students.

Motivating Phrases

Occasionally, during the lesson, you need to create a little suspense to break the rhythm and reactivate attention. We can do it in so many ways, even with simple motivating phrases like "now, guys, be careful because the beauty is coming!" or "attention, please, because this concept is beautiful" or "is new," "is exceptional." Also, the motivating phrase goes to solicit the self-esteem of the guys. "What I am about to present to you now is for you, who are smart and intuitive kids, a very simple concept (an explanation, information, etc.)."

Motivating phrases need to be reinforced with para verbal codes and nonverbal. The aim is to create expectations or leverage self-esteem to prepare the kids to welcome an important step in the lesson or simply to draw attention. This technique can be used even if, in reality, the concept or the fact that we explain is far from interesting or very important, but with the aim, as said, to reactivate the attention.

Make concrete examples and urge the creation of mental images. Urge in detail the creation of mental images during an explanation, for example of Roman history: "imagine, boys, this Roman soldier, handsome, tall, sturdy, still dressed in his white tunic, long to the knee, and holding the sword, who comes to his house, looks at his field and sees his garden full of nettles, etc."

The whole dramatized with para-verbal and nonverbal, reactivates the attention and makes more clear and understandable a historical process characterized by cause-effect relationships. But, inviting and accustoming students to create mental images even when they have to study helps them to develop a more efficient method of study and to abandon the mnemonic study of content to learn.

Affiliate Humor

Psychologists argue that a comical-humorous attitude within the group, in general, can only establish a climate suitable for the development of curiosity, exploration, attention, and consequently to prepare to give effective and positive responses in the learning processes. Not only that. The positive and benevolent wit joke encourages friendships, bonding, emotional stability, psychological and social wellbeing, higher and significant levels of self-esteem, improves the quality of relationships. In class, the simple joke or comic-humorous story, proposed by the teacher, allows to take a recreational break; it allows everyone, teacher and students, to unload the possible tensions or, to prepare for a new phase of concentration and school commitment. It is not a question of appearing superficial and frivolous, on the contrary: it is a question of using communicative techniques capable of changing the mood itself within the class.

A joke of the teacher can be very useful to indicate, with more lightness, mistakes and wrong behaviors: thus, the same reproach can wear the clothes of hilarity that, a lot, affects much more effectively than a real direct warning.

STRATEGIES FOR EFFECTIVE ONLINE COMMUNICATION

You can see the communication gap and how it can easily create both misunderstanding and confusion. So how do you make up for that gap? Here are four practices that will go a long way to make your online communication clear and effective.

Use Emoticons and Use Them Often

For some reason, our tendency as humans is to read things in a negative light. Emoticons help to mitigate that dynamic, and they help you to convey the more positive aspects of communication, such as encouragement, openness, and compassion.

Communicate Often

Imagine a face-to-face course where the professor shows up late for class. The first week she's five minutes late, the second week it's fifteen minutes. What would be the fallout? Her students would begin to disengage, and she would see empty seats marking the curious absence of several students. The same principle is at work in your online course: if your students feel like you are absent, they are more likely to disengage. When you model attention and presence, you should witness an increase in participation.

Address Students by Name

The word we enjoy seeing and hearing most is our own name. When an instructor begins her correspondence or grading comments with our name, we take notice; it communicates that we are seen as a real person who matters. This is an easy way to make your students more receptive and more engaged, but it's an easy practice to forget. Make it one of your habits.

CHAPTER - 16

BUILDING CONNECTION

For you to connect with your students very well, your students must love you and find your course appealing. It will be difficult to connect with someone that doesn't like your course. There are effective ways that you can connect with your students very well. The best way to connect with your students is to;

DAILY PRACTICES TO BUILD A CONNECTION

The first goal of online classes is to attract and engage students, which is still a daunting task for most teachers. The Internet has given us the right tools to simplify our work. Once you have thought about finding the right forum and creating online classes, you need to design your curriculum so that it is focused and committed to your students.

It takes a little extra work to find out why students get involved in social media or what they read online. This basic tool helps you connect with students, and sometimes these classroom references (with memoranda or examples) help them learn and memorize concepts. Students always respond positively to someone who understands them, so first learn what you like.

Preparation of new teaching materials

The Internet offers people easy access to the vast amount of information they expect to be discovered. List the front pages of the course and regularly search for new topics that students may find helpful.

When preparing your curriculum, consider the following:

Introduce the audience

Before you start an online course, it is good to know the names of the students. Plan a week and contact each student to learn about their history and interests.

If an appointment is not possible, order online group chats to connect. This way, you will understand the students during the course, and you will need to set learning objectives before preparing a plan for each lesson.

Create emotional content for your students

Students respond better by explaining concepts with examples that may be emotionally related to each other. Managing these memorable moments makes it easier for them to remember difficult concepts.

Example: Almost all online students attending European football are passionate about football. So to explain the concept of linguistics, I now include in my notes a serious accident that occurred over the weekend.

Add nice graphics

It's almost boring to move back and forth between text slips in the classroom. Here you have to present something funny, like an image .gif, a meme or a short film, a 1-minute harvest, etc. And when students practice questions, they can use a fun timer to set the calculation.

Remember the concepts with cards and games

A license card is a very useful tool to facilitate student attraction and review. In the online environment, many features make traditional maps more useful.

Take an interactive quiz every week

Another purpose of online learning is to get students into exams as they look a little away from their desks. To make this interesting and keep students untouched, you can play a fun quiz while answering questions.

With the help of a weekly quiz, students can always review and direct courses, which is very important for ESL students. By participating in challenging quizzes, learning can be easy and fun for young students.

Build Real Teacher-Student Connections

Eligible online educators often worry that virtual teaching is more about making a good learning experience and not just about the mechanics of distance learning—no matter what the setting of learning is. Despite that, getting to know their students is very challenging for some online teachers. This happens when an online class has 20 and above students at a time. So, if the course is online, with no eye to eye connections, then how can you build individual connections? All things considered, there are various proven ways to work around the issue. I pulled up some of them to help you navigate building connections with your students.

As an online instructor, building a strong connection with your students is crucial because there is no visual aid to help you see all of them at once during a class, and while a couple of the students in the class are noisy, the rest of them may stay quiet. What this means is that it is easy for you to overlook the students who are not actively communicating.

Thus, it turns out to be extremely difficult for you to know which student is doing some other thing, sleeping, incapable of seeing the course layout, or just generally lost. This happens in an online course that neglects to include an important learning key, i.e., personal connection with the instructor.

Also, without an important connection with you, your students can get confused and may feel detached. This makes them less motivated, and they begin to lose interest in the course.

Introductions

Most online courses include a type of early introduction, for example, a conversation discussion that expects students to post something important to them, as a way of getting to know one another better.

Discussion Boards

This may not be possible to react to each student's post each week. This methodology isn't really attractive, either. They may give you another way of concentrating on different individual students every week.

Email

All over your course, there are various points when you or your students have to start an email discussion. This can be a good way to check on a student when you notice there have not been active, or he or she is missing assignments.

Make it meaningful

A personal connection with your students is a higher priority than creative conversations. Everyone is occupied with responsibilities of work, school, and family, so adding prerequisites for connection for the sake of just adding them is counterproductive.

Consider class size and time

Be realistic about what you can achieve, given the number of students in your course and the amount of time you need to work with them. Large registrations, as well as shorter learning times, make individual connections nearly impossible. Alter your expectations appropriately and consider what you can do with little groups to cultivate a connection and communication.

Plan ahead

Make plans to learn and adapt to both you and your students and continue because of clear communication systems.

Practice

Challenge yourself to make these individual connections yet allow time for slow adaptation. Start gradually with new methods to know what works for you and your students, and don't be hesitant to get some information about their interests and expectations as well. The same way you adjust your content and materials before every lesson, you can also try new ways to deal with communication.

Introduce Yourself

Create a feeling of cooperation and connection between your students and yourself by starting the first conversation. Try to make this meeting by inspiring conversation as far as learning and individual goals of students, their strengths, and other additional characteristics.

You can begin by posting a short bio of yourself. This may include your area of specialization, background, interests, and your most recent photograph. This will make your students feel that you are a good teacher, and they will follow your example and use it as an aid to guide them in sharing information about themselves with the rest of the class.

This is one of the best ways to connect with the students in your online classroom and to know their interests. You can also use Google Forms to gather information on your students, find out about their interests, their background, their educational abilities, and their learning preferences. Another smart idea is to dedicate a particular part of your course site for posting pictures and brief profiles of all of your students.

Or then again, even better, you can ask your students to create a quick personal mindset board that they can share with you and the rest of the class. For this, you ask them to use a few accessible online mindset mapping instruments.

Adapt Your Course

One of the best ways to amplify the individual connection and to expand the capability of eLearning is to adapt your course. When we say adapt the course, we mean structure it in a way that incorporates human connection.

An adapted course is bound to establish a relationship between you and ng way

Influence Online Conversations

Give the students a conversation platform. Providing an online conversation board contributes to relating with friends and fellow students and in getting important feedback. Because of this, the best choice is to go with an online platform that you are familiar with—one which is easily reachable to your students. Also, you can use the conversation boards' tool, or perhaps you can create a Facebook group and ask your students to join.

Advance Multimedia with Personalization

Media fused courses empower the various kinds of students to meet their personal needs. Various students have diverse learning styles, so the most ideal approach to furnishing them with reasonable learning resources is through sight and sound. You may utilize YouTube and assist visual students with videos. Also, give a digital podcast to students who learn better with sound and intuitive games for students who do better through gamification of learning.

But, if you wish to get intuitive and precise feedback, you should make video updates and video presentations on your course. These videos may include:

Discussions concerning the next week's assignments and its specific subtleties. Additionally, best practices and questions from students regarding different assignments.

Discussions about the lessons of the past week or any information which needs any update or support.

More information to the primary content: some industry-based tips and hacks.

You could make on-the-spot learning through VoiceThread, for your students to be able to collaborate with you and each other during interpretation.

All of this will help in keeping your audiovisual course fascinating, and it will also help in improving your students' understanding.

Foster Collaborative Learning

This teaching strategy is a brilliant method to increase the motivation of students to learn. This happens through group learning. In this teaching strategy, a little group of students collaborates on a specific project or task.

Henceforth, the responsibility for and teaching is shared by the group of students. This gives your students substantially more chances to actively take part in their learning, in asking questions, and in evaluating one another. Besides, your students will show signs of improvement and willingness to share; they will talk about their thoughts directly and apply what they have learned and are learning.

If you design the exercises carefully, you can help your students learn the skills they need to effectively work as a team. These organized conversations additionally help to avoid arguments and fights.

Another way to avoid these contentions is to encourage your students to speak with one another and to have important conversations. Also, create a classroom that would promote a safe platform for meaningful and attentive conversations—including questions to offer ascent to result-oriented arguments.

Engage Them in Decision Making

Nothing could be more empowering than permitting an individual to become a part of important decision-making processes. While this is a typical practice in the business world to enable workers to feel drawn in, the same practice can also be used in building stronger connections with your online students. So, let your students partake in the decision-making process of the class. For example, allow them to pick the projects which they will do or the specific points which you will examine in a personal essay. The most important thing is that you make them feel they are a real part of the online teaching course. To do this, you can make use of Survey Monkey to find out about students' supposition, or you may simply add a few evaluations to your eLearning course. Additionally, if you have Slack, you could also use Polly application for your review arrangements.

Support Intelligent Communication

The most direct way to promote connection is to support intelligent communication. This may include texting or live chats.

Encourage your students to benefit as much as possible from whatever form of intelligent conversations you all decide on, whether it is moderated conversations or off and on conversations. Encourage them to leverage on this opportunity to connect you as well as with their schoolmates, concerning their project conversations or group projects.

Define Your Student Reward System

Prizes are a great way to keep your students motivated. It causes them to be more interested in the course, helping them to focus on learning. Since individuals acknowledge rewards, a lot of teachers benefit as much as possible from remunerations systems to get the attention of their students. These prizes can be given at the end of projects or group exercises.

Another approach to connect with your students is to consider their suggestions when choosing the prize. An award for finishing the course of action will persuade your students to invest greater energy in learning, and they will consistently stay connected with you and focused on the course's goals.

As an online instructor, all your students need to have the most ideal learning involvement with your courses. A personal connection between you and a student can influence their levels of commitment, as well as information retention and success. Creating opportunities for personalized communication and building a connection, while both basic parts of online teaching, are not the same. Personalized communication is only one way to build positive connections with your online students.

Appreciate your Students

You might not like it because you see it as degrading yourself. That's wrong. This tip works like magic. Always appreciate your students. Tell them how happy you are seeing them online. Try to recognize their presence. Whether you are doing prerecording or live video, always appreciate your students. If you know their names, you can mention them one by one. When you appreciate your students, they will love you more. They will feel comfortable sharing their problems with you.

Motivate your students

It is another factor that most tutors overlook when teaching online. But it is a crucial factor that you need to put into practice. You are teaching a distant student who you don't know the life experiences he is facing. Most students study harder when someone inspires them. Be a motivator to your students. When you are teaching, use the avenue to motivate your students.

Listen

Listen to your student's problems, ideas, or contributions. What you are doing is teaching some set of people online. You are not teaching ghosts. So, allow them to ask their questions, and you reply to them. Giving your students a listening ear will help them to understand your course quickly.

Create an Online community

It is another way to connect with your students. Most tutors add forums on their website where the students will communicate, crake joke with one another. Creating a community will ease every unnecessary pressure that the students are facing in a particular course. Your online community will also allow the students to share ideas, a solution to questions.

Give assignment that enables Students to Share their Experiences

Giving students a task that allows them to share their experience will also help you to connect with your students. The assignments can be essay writing, history projects, or anything – depending on your course.

Create a Classroom Environment That Helps Students Feel Connected

A narrative approach to teaching will help you create a classroom environment that keeps students engaged. Talk about yourself, tell stories, and create fun learning opportunities for students while being online. Call students by their names, remember any kind of detail about them, and create stories during the different lessons to help you create a fun and comfortable classroom environment.

CHAPTER - 17

DEVELOPING AS AN
ONLINE INSTRUCTOR

SET GOALS FOR ONLINE STUDENTS

Check the Progress of Online Students

For short-term progress checks, be sure to create continuity between lessons by making quick reviews or quizzes on previous topics. A great way to remind students of their long-term progress is to build a working portfolio with them so they can look back and see how far they have gone. One way to do this online is to start a results page. While teaching young students, every time they do something, go to the achievement page and ask them to draw something which represents what they have learned (you may want to turn it into an achievement tree that they can add too or a trophy shelf). With teenagers or adults, you may prefer asking them to write something. As the course progresses, the page fills with success reminders and moments of pride for your students.

Visuals

If your students can see you through a webcam, make sure the background area does look not only presentable but also neat. The same applies to your appearance. While appearance is critical, the way you interact with students is of paramount importance, since you have to give them your full attention and avoid looking busy doing other stuff. Also, the visuals must be up to par, so make sure the slides or any content are clean and clear and that all the videos you use are of good quality.

WAYS TO BETTER KNOW YOUR STUDENTS

Here's a typical experience from my many years as a commuter student in college and graduate school.

Use a Hardcopy of Student Groups or Class Lists

Early in the semester, print off a sheet of each of your groups. If your course is not organized by groups, then print off your entire class list. Before you do, be sure to sort your students alphabetically. Most learning management systems will include your students' photos and email addresses.

Checking-in Emails

Periodically, click into your participant's list and look for students who haven't logged in for several days (you can do this by sorting your students by the last login). Send them an email. It may appear that they are not engaging the course, but it could mean that something else is going on. Oftentimes, they are dealing with an illness or a family situation and are feeling stressed about the course.

This is a perfect time to connect with and support them. It takes just a few minutes, but often this makes a big difference in the life of the student.

PATHWAYS FOR YOUR SUCCESS

Unquestionably, teaching online is a lot of work. Online teaching requires you to motivate your students with logic and reason rather than with a gregarious personality. Online teaching requires you to preplan everything as bird-walk, Storytime just doesn't happen as it does in a face-to-face class. And, if you're not careful, it can become too much work and keep you for doing the equally valuable, if not more valuable, things your annual performance review requires of you.

How do you keep from working late into the night and letting your online teaching consume your entire weekend? Just like students need structures and checklists, so do you.

Eye Contact and Appearance

Make eye contact with your students by looking directly into the camera or at least near your camera. Looking directly into the camera can feel strange at first and easy to forget. A helpful trick is to draw a smiley face or get a smiley face sticker and stick it on your computer next to the camera. It's silly, but it works.

Arrive Early

Just as you arrive early to prepare for your on-campus classroom, plan to sign in early to your online Zoom classroom. Use this time to prepare and open any documents for screen sharing, test your equipment, and converse with students who come to class early. Compared to most classrooms, the Zoom classroom is technically complicated. By getting in early, you simplify things, creating a margin for yourself and space to connect with your students.

Be Ready for the Worst

Know how to mute your students' microphones and how to shut down their video stream. Think of this as knowing where to get the fire extinguisher in case there is a fire. Like extinguishing fires, muting participants should not become a regular practice. However, we need to know how to shut things down quickly when encountering the rare circumstance of a student and spouse argument or a student who has thought they turned off their camera and is changing their clothes.

Provide a Single Entrance to Your Classroom

Provide your students with one link to your online Zoom meeting that they can revisit for every meeting in their semester, quarter, etc. Scheduling multiple meetings takes unnecessary work and creates confusion.

CHAPTER - 18

WHAT'S THE MOST

IMPORTANT THING?

INSTRUCTOR PARTICIPATION

Reading as many discussion board posts as you can and responding to them promptly is recommended. When students know you are actively participating, they are more likely to take responsibility for how they contribute to the online class.

Timing is Everything

You can imagine what happens when an instructor only replies to discussions at the very end of the week. Only a few students view the instructor comments and even fewer respond. This is because learners have moved on to the next week's work. It's like last Sunday's newspaper; the readership has disappeared. So, timing is everything. Engage your students' discussion posts during the day when their initial posts are due or on the day after. For example, if the first post is due on Wednesday, reply to them on Wednesday or Thursday.

A note on instructor summary posts

These are posts the instructor writes after the discussion is over; in them, the professor sums up the discussion and makes some final comments. Summary posts do have their benefits; however, you run up against the same issue of timing. So, if you write a summary post, send it out as an email to the entire class. This way, you're guaranteed that your students will see it. Better yet, have your students create their own summary posts.

A note on requiring posts

I have strong opinions on this subject. If you want participation, then your discussions will need teeth; that means some form of evaluation. That may mean peer evaluations, grading each discussion, or an overall semester or quarter grade for discussion participation and post quality. Because grading discussions can be more subjective, rubrics become helpful for both the instructor and students.

Be Clear on Your Purpose

Before you begin responding to your students, spend some time getting oriented. Read over the discussion prompt and ask yourself, "What's the goal of this discussion?" or "What's the learning outcome I'm trying to facilitate?" This gives you a framework and a focus as you respond.

If you're looking for an area of focus for your own professional development, facilitating threaded discussions would be a great place to spend your time and energy. It's usually the most dynamic and interactive part of an online course, and you can get incredibly creative with these by using role-play, case studies, and student-to-student interviews.

YOUR HEART NEEDS FRIENDS & FAMILY

In addition to you needing to be building your CV, nurturing a professional network, and exercising your body, I don't want you to forget about your spiritual heart and soul. Eschewing politically correct and inclusive terms for a moment, nobody likes a "dull boy" because a "dull boy" has nothing of interest to talk about besides their work. I am certain that you are not a dull boy, and I don't want anyone to think that about you. But that happens to stay-at-home academics all too often, and I don't wish that for you.

You shouldn't be working on academic work all the time. It is not healthy. And it is not fair to you. At some level, working all of the time is disrespectful to yourself, your friends, your pets, and your family. And, if you're the spiritual type, it certainly isn't the only reason that some omnipotent being put you on this Earth. You have something to contribute to your family, your community, your country, and your universe, and it is more than spending a gazillion hours teaching your college classes.

Get a hobby

Academics at large are extremely high risk for being boring individuals. They either talk incessantly about the things they are interested in or don't know what to say. You've probably heard it said that experts know more and more about less and less until they know everything there is to know about nothing. Does that sound like someone you would like to hang out with socially?

If you don't have an enthusiastic answer when someone asks you what your hobbies are, you are in trouble. Boring people say that they do not have enough time to have hobbies unless they are parents of quintuplets or some other such blessing. You need to make time for a hobby of some kind—cool your overworked brain by focusing on something else occasionally, which incidentally will encourage you to become a more interesting individual. Don't know where to start? Try an Internet search for something akin to "I need a new hobby."

Read newspaper headlines but not articles

You also need people in your life to remind you that there is more to life than just your laptop computer. Stay-at-home academic or not, academics are too often notably poor conversationalists. This leads to awkward moments of silence when sitting in a virtual zoom on google hangout meeting room waiting for everyone to arrive. How do you fill the uncomfortable void when there isn't anything to talk about?

It is worth taking take 30 seconds of each day when starting your computer up to quickly note that day's newspaper or web newsfeed headlines. However, what is different here is that the smart stay-at-home academic never actually reads the articles following the headlines. In this way, you can break awkward silences by revealing that you noticed a headline earlier in the day but haven't yet had time to read the accompanying article and are curious if anyone else in the around the virtual tables knows what the story is all about. This strategy almost always gets a conversation going and grants you the appearance of a great conversationalist while letting other folks feel good about themselves by telling you what they know.

Host a monthly spaghetti dinner party

A moratorium on groups of people getting together won't last forever, but your reputation as a stay-at-home academic will last quite a while, mostly because you will get to be so good at it!

Just like you need to purposefully make time for your specific academic tasks, you also need to purposefully make time to nurture relationships with other human beings. When you were in elementary school, friendships just seemed to naturally happen; as an adult, friendships are more difficult to come by. Adult friendships need to be intentionally sought after and frequently nurtured, particularly in the academic world where people move across the country frequently.

The easiest way to start a circle of friends is to be on the alert for four people from four different segments of your life and invite them to your house for a casual spaghetti dinner. A box of spaghetti and a can of pasta sauce only costs a few dollars, and when served comes with few expectations. You can even open a cheap jug of red wine if you are so inclined.

CONCLUSION

Although online learning has been around for many decades, the world had not appreciated its relevance until the moment that there was a global need for it. This has been the best time for us to adopt the existing education methods in ways that don't require the students and teachers to have physical contact before knowledge is imparted. By making use of the available resources online, our children can stay home during any period of isolation and enjoy their learning. Online learning can help to create a form of engagement with the students and prevent them from experiencing mental isolation.

This book remains a valuable guide that helps to show the way to keep our minds at work by using technology as an alternative rather than succumbing to the situation around us.